BUCKAROO HEART

BUCKAROO
HEART

❧❧

Rick Steber

Bonanza Publishing

ISBN: 0-945134-32-0

Bonanza Publishing
Box 204
Prineville, Oregon 97754

Cover design by Gary Asher – Maverick Publications

Printed in the USA

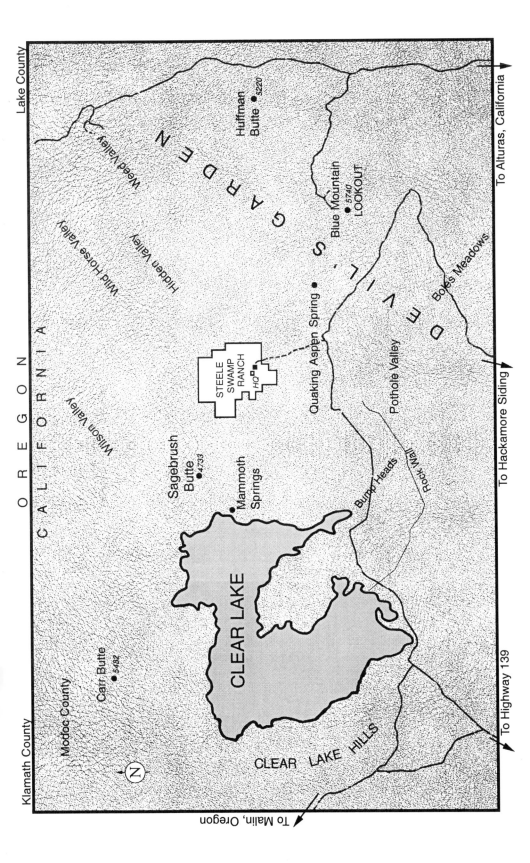

BOOKS BY RICK STEBER

Rendezvous
Traces
Where Rolls the Oregon
Heartwood
Oregon Trail – The Last of the Pioneers
Roundup
New York to Nome
Wild Horse Rider
The Tales of the Wild West Series
Oregon Trail
Pacific Coast
Indians
Cowboys
Women of the West
Children's Stories
Loggers
Mountain Men
Miners
Grandpa's Stories
Pioneers
Campfire Stories
Tall Tales
Gunfighters
Grandma's Stories

DEDICATION

For Charles and Bettye Steber, Jim and Pat Ottoman,
Nondice McFall and Charlie West

ACKNOWLEDGMENTS

With special thanks to Kristi Steber, Gary Asher, Brian Gardner, Patrick Brock, Skip Cosper, Wade Martin, Kevin O'Brien, Jerry Scdoris, Ron Harpole and Dr. Don Sutherland. Also, my sincere appreciation to all the family and friends of Herman, Betty and Ray Vowell who so graciously shared their remembrances and stories: Susan Vowell, Dr. Jack Martin, Dr. Ray Tice, Barney Weaver, Rachel Stockwell, Ed Donavan, Mike Morgan, Lee Manildi, Dorothy Sundberg, Faye Thompson, Ina Addington, Erma Fairclo and Norman Bettendorf.

PHOTOGRAPHS

FOREWORD

Herman Vowell pulled the blankets up and tenderly tucked them around Betty's shoulders. The heater clicked on, metal groaned in expansion and hot air spewed forth like the breath of a fairy-tale dragon. A fast-moving storm passed through and lightning flashed across the wild night sky, illuminating in eerie white bursts the photograph on the night stand. Captured within the simple frame was an image of Betty on the day she had been crowned queen of the Madrone rodeo. It was Herman's most treasured possession. He had put it under glass in the hope it would last forever.

While the storm raged Herman relived the life he had shared with Betty on the secluded ranch in the Devil's Garden. Betty was the center of each memory; the ringlets of her soft brown hair falling nearly to her shoulders, her eyes green and translucent as an ocean wave, her smile so happy, radiant, infectious.

Tears rolled down Herman's leathery cheeks and he did not wipe them away. When he finally spoke his voice was distant and brittle as he sobbed out each syllable, "You're so beautiful." Herman took Betty's hand and squeezed it. There was no response. He bent and kissed her cool forehead. And then he just held her as he desperately clung to the hope that the strength of his love, and the sheer force of his will, would somehow keep his wife alive through the night. Fear gripped him hard and full. Time passed. At last there were no more tears for him to cry.

Slowly Herman became conscious of movement. Of a touch. Betty's thumb was moving against the back of his hand, softly rubbing, caressing. In a raspy whisper she told him, "I do love you, Herman." And a moment later, "What we have will last forever."

The moon, the guardian of the night, found a hole between clouds and sent a silver shaft of light toward earth. Herman breathed, "Darling, I knew you'd never leave me."

ONE

F rom a high point in the Devil's Garden you can sit in your
saddle and see into three states; north to Yainax Butte in
Oregon, south to the snowy summit of California's Mount Shasta,
and east to the saw-toothed profile of the Warner Mountains of
northwestern Nevada.

The Devil's Garden is good country; a mile-high plateau of
sagebrush flats cut by long fingers of ponderosa pine, interspersed by
swales of waving green grasses fed by springs that defy logic and
unexpectedly boil forth, run for a ways, and disappear into the red
volcanic soil. Littering this vast landscape are chunks of black
basaltic rock that seem to have been randomly scattered by the devil
himself.

Across this open rangeland roam herds of wild mustangs. Mule
deer and antelope winter here and each spring and fall great flocks of
waterfowl, following ancient migration routes, pass noisily
overhead. Nowhere in this remote expanse is there any sign of a fence

or a boundary; nor, in fact, can the hand of man be seen except for a ranch or two, a few meager roads and the occasional buckaroo who moves across the lonely panorama in pursuit of the grazing cattle.

The names of the landmarks sing the song of the Devil's Garden: Rock Creek, Quaking Aspen Spring, Blue Mountain, Pothole Valley, Mammoth Spring, Clear Lake, Sagebrush Butte, Round Valley, Dobie Swale, Beaver Mountain, Dry Lake, Wild Horse Camp, Hackamore Siding, Saddle Blanket Flat, Coyote Butte, Horse Mountain, Mud Lake, Hopeless Pass, Willow Creek, Dead Horse Flat, Lost River....

The isolation of Steele Swamp Ranch was never a concern to Betty Vowell, not even when they were snowbound for months at a time. But for several days before the big storm of March 24, 1948 she had a sense of uneasiness and even dread. One moment she would feel chilled, a while later feverish, and there was the constant and peculiar discomfort that rode low in her belly. She began to fear for the life of the baby growing inside her.

The morning after the big storm Betty was washing breakfast dishes and longing for the company of another woman, someone who had experienced motherhood and could reassure her that these aches and pains were normal. She glanced up from her work and took comfort in seeing her husband Herman driving the hay sled past the window, breaking a trail through the eighteen inches of fresh snow. His brother Ray slid down from the top of the load and opened the gate, pushing the impatient cows away so Herman could drive through. As Betty washed the pots and pans and wiped down the counter top she occasionally looked in their direction and saw the work team pull the sled in a large circle while the two men forked hay onto the ground and the cows crowded around in their wake.

A sudden wave of nausea swept over Betty. She tried to convince herself that the little rascal in her tummy was the cause. Such feelings were normal, she thought. Then a stab of intense pain, as sharp as a jagged knife thrust into her belly, stole her breath. Instinctively, as if to protect her baby, she doubled over, riding the icy edge of agony. She managed to suck in a breath and when the pain eased a little she snatched a dish towel off the rack. Salty tears stung her eyes. It was her intent to step out the door, into the glaring sunlight, and wave that cheerfully colored dish towel in an anguished attempt to catch Herman or Ray's attention.

Betty never knew if she was able to accomplish her mission. Later all she could remember was clutching the towel and grabbing the edge of the counter to keep from falling, hanging there for a few precarious seconds while pieces of a black jig-saw puzzle came wheeling toward her; pieces floating, colliding, locking in place. And when the puzzle was complete she lost consciousness and slumped to the linoleum floor where she lay face down, motionless. There was no more worry, no more pain, no more fear of losing her baby.

Earlier that morning, as Betty stood at the wood stove cooking breakfast, Herman had noticed the way she abruptly fingered her side, as if she had a catch there. He slid off his chair and in stocking feet walked to her and touched her arm. Her skin felt cool and he quietly asked, "Everything okay?"

She had managed a tight-lipped smile. "A little twinge," she said, "that's all."

"Mornin'," Ray called, as he strolled into the kitchen from his bedroom.

Herman and Betty returned the greeting. Their moment together was interrupted but it probably did not matter. Betty was funny that way. If she felt under the weather she hid the fact, never letting on, believing those around her deserved to see her cheery side and nothing less.

Betty served breakfast and Herman was still watching as she gingerly bent to pull the biscuits out of the oven. She spooned bacon and eggs onto their plates. To him she looked thin, pale, tired. Maybe that was the way women started a pregnancy. If she had been a mare or a heifer he would have known.

On the way out the door Herman gave her a quick kiss on the cheek and made his way toward the barn. All the sounds of his world lay muted under the fresh layer of wet snow; the thousand head of cows on the meadow bellowing their hunger, the barking dogs behind him, the scolding magpie that had come near to look for a handout but settled for picking through fresh horse manure. Herman speculated about the baby while he followed the trail Ray had broken. How was its arrival going to change his life? He hoped the baby would be born in late August, preferably after haying. Herman wondered if he would still be able to compete at the rodeo in Alturas, California. He had won there two years running, saddle bronc in '46 and calf roping in '47.

As he neared the barn he paused for a moment, drinking in the aroma of the work horses and listening to his shy brother speak to them with soft and gentle words. "How we feeling today? Lot of snow. Got your work cut out for you. Move over a smidgen, there, easy now...." Herman savored the subtle sounds the horses made, the soft swish of their tails moving the air, lower lips rubbing feed boxes, teeth grinding the rolled oats, hooves clattering. All of it was music to his ears.

Herman stepped around the corner and asked his brother, "Ready to roll?"

"Ready as I'll ever be," responded Ray. He tugged on the halters of two Belgian work horses, leading them through the open door and positioning them in front of the loaded hay sled parked under the protected overhang of the barn. The cows in the field had been watching and with this sure sign they were about to be fed, they began bawling in earnest and surging like a brown tide in the direction of the gate.

"Glad I insisted we load up last night," called Herman.

"You said it wasn't gonna snow. Remember?"

"Naw. You were the one said it was gonna blow on through."

Herman climbed over the bunk and picked up the lines.

Ray chuckled. He did not mind allowing his younger brother the last word. Herman could talk for days, interrupting himself only to draw a quick breath between stories. One time at a rodeo someone had asked how he could find the Vowell brothers and was told, "Just listen and you'll know where to find Herman. Ray, you'll have to hunt for him." Herman was always going to have the last word. That was just the way it was.

Ray fastened the last tug to the harness and climbed to the top of the load of slippery hay. As they jerked into motion he noticed a flock of Canada geese passing overhead, noisily protesting that the swamp, where they traditionally rested on the way north, was covered with snow. Ray was watching the geese make one lazy turn after another in the tall blue sky when he was surprised to realize the sled had stopped and Herman was patiently waiting for him to get down and open the gate.

As he passed in front of the sled Herman called above the noise of the cattle, "Little early for daydreaming."

"Never too early."

As the gate swung open Herman's thoughts drifted to Betty and the special secret they shared; soon there would be a telltale bulge in her belly, a baby growing there, his baby, their baby. Ray did not know yet, but they were planning to tell him in the next few days.

"You look like the cat that swallowed the canary," Ray commented, as Herman drove through.

Herman just grinned. In the six years he and Betty had been married they had come to the conclusion they would never have children. And then six weeks before, on Valentine's Day, Betty's 28th birthday, Herman and Betty were alone in the kitchen. She was washing dishes. He was drying. She shook the suds off her hands, turned to Herman, wrapped her arms around his thin waist and impulsively told him, "I do love you, Sugarplum."

He responded, "Well, I love you, too."

Betty whispered that she had missed her period, expecting

him to discern her deeper meaning.

"You did?"

"I think," she had said, "we might be pregnant."

Herman took her pretty face in his rough hands and kissed her full on the lips. He knew they would raise the baby at the remote ranch in the Devil's Garden and for a fleeting moment he envisioned himself hoisting a son onto the saddle, his first horseback ride, leading the horse in a circle around the corral. Betty snuggled tightly against Herman's chest and they clung to each other. The two happiest people alive.

The brothers were nearly finished feeding the first load of hay when Herman's attention was drawn away from the cattle and up the long hill to the low-slung house. There was no reason for Herman to look in the direction of the house except for his overriding concern for Betty. A vague image of a woman appeared on the porch, frantically waving something, a towel perhaps. Forever after, that strange portrait would be etched in Herman's mind, along with the unspoken truth it represented; that at any instant in a man's life everything he loves, treasures and holds dearest to his heart can be stolen away from him.

The moment Herman caught sight of the apparition he blurted out, "Something's wrong!" His first inclination was that the house was on fire but he saw a straight line of lazy smoke rising from the chimney and then it hit him, "It's Betty!"

Ray grabbed the lines and urged the team forward but they could not go fast enough to suit Herman and he leaped from the sled and ran toward the house. By the time he reached the porch his leg muscles were on fire and he was breathing in great gulps of air. He threw open the door and charged inside, a trail of snow following him to the point where he discovered his dear wife lying face down on the kitchen floor, a dish towel beside her. He dropped to one knee and his first thought was that she had stumbled, hit her head and knocked herself dizzy. He touched her shoulder, spoke to her, "Betty. Betty. Can you hear me? Betty!"

A jolt of panic hit him and he tried to move, tried to touch her face but he could not will his muscles to obey. He was frozen, remembering how pale she appeared at breakfast, knowing that he should have done something then; had her sit down, put her to bed, something, anything.

Ray was there. "What happened?"

Very gently Herman rolled her over, scooped her up in his arms and stood, telling Ray, "Turn back the covers." He carried her to the bedroom and gently laid her down. He removed her slippers, pulled the covers up to her chest and stood back and looked at her. Her skin was so white it looked luminescent and the muscles in her face were as relaxed as if she were merely sleeping.

Ray, who adored Betty, asked in a subdued voice, "She going to be all right, Herman?"

It was then that the full reality of the predicament hit Herman. Here they were, snowbound, at one of the most isolated ranches in North America, more than 70 miles away from the nearest doctor. Betty was unconscious. They had to find someone with medical training who could come and help.

"Stay with her," Herman said. "I'll try and get out on the phone."

Herman cranked the wall phone and when the operator finally came on the line he muttered, "Thank God."

"Is that you, Herman? Morning," said Rita Smerl cheerfully. She was sitting in an office in Alturas, 53 miles away. "I can't believe those old lines out to Steele Swamp held up in that storm. Must be your lucky day. So what can I do for you, Herman?"

"Rita," said Herman drawing a breath and then, fearing the connection might go dead at any moment, he charged ahead. "We got ourselves a situation out here. Betty's unconscious. We need a doctor in the worst way."

"How's anybody going to get there? The roads won't be open for days, maybe weeks," said Rita.

"I don't know but we've got to do something, and fast. She don't look good, Rita."

"I'll check around. Maybe Mervyn Wilde can help. He's the head of Search and Rescue for Klamath County. Stay near the phone. I'll get back to you just as soon as I can. And Herman, if the line goes dead and I can't get you, I want you to know, we'll do everything we can for Betty. Talk to you soon."

Herman stood for a long moment. He did not want to hang up and break the connection between the ranch and the outside world. Finally he did. He went straight to Betty.

Thelma Archer, the wife of the manager at Willow Creek Ranch, was the nearest neighbor to the Vowells. When Herman rang the operator, Thelma was listening on the party line. It was customary for neighbors to do so and was one of their few forms of entertainment. Thelma eavesdropped on Herman's conversation and she picked up again when Rita called back to tell Herman that an airplane, outfitted with skis, would fly the new doctor in Malin to the ranch. As soon as Thelma knew help was on its way she left a note for her husband. "Ernest, Gone to Steele Swamp. Betty's real sick. Be back when I can get here. Love, Thelma." She went to the barn, saddled a horse and rode toward Steele Swamp, twenty miles away.

TWO

It was fate that brought Dr. Jack Martin to the town of Malin, Oregon. He grew up on a farm near Topeka, Kansas and graduated from the University of Kansas. He was three months into his surgical residency at St. Mary's Hospital in Kansas City when the Army called him into active duty. He was stationed at Camp McCoy in Sparta, Wisconsin when the war ended and, as the last medical officer on duty, he was given the assignment to close down the hospital. He packed 30 foot lockers with medical supplies and equipment that he would need in private practice, painted an X in white paint on the end of each box and took them to the surplus warehouse. The following day he returned and offered a dollar for every foot locker with an X painted on the end. Jack loaded the foot lockers into an old milk van and the next morning, he and his wife LaVon headed west. Jack loved hunting and fishing and thought the Northwest would be a good place for them to live and work.

Jack had hoped to settle in Bend, Oregon, where the hunting

and fishing were legendary, but when they arrived a prominent doctor informed him that the medical community in Bend was closed to outsiders. "We can't stop you from living here," he told Dr. Martin, "but we can guarantee you will never be given hospital privileges. If you try to set up a practice here you will starve. If you wish to continue in the field of medicine it would be my recommendation you travel on."

About 200 miles south, the small farm town of Malin, populated mainly by Czechoslovakian immigrants, was in desperate need of a local physician. Dr. Martin and LaVon found Malin to their liking and moved into a small home provided by the Kalina family. Dr. Martin began his practice on March 2, 1948, in an office across from his home. He unpacked his foot lockers, unlocked the door and waited for business. Most people in the community were used to driving to Klamath Falls, 30 miles away, for any major illness or injury. His patients generally suffered from minor colds, headaches, bunions and arthritis.

On the morning of March 25 Dr. Martin awoke to discover more than a foot of snow had fallen. He followed the snow plow to Klamath Falls to check on his patients who were hospitalized there. When he returned to Malin he found a man waiting for him outside his office. The man introduced himself as Mervyn Wilde, head of Klamath County Search and Rescue.

"We've got an emergency," Mervyn told him. "A woman at one of the ranches out in the Devil's Garden might be dying. I've arranged for a small plane to fly you there. Can you be ready in fifteen minutes?"

"Not so fast." Dr. Martin did not enjoy flying in small airplanes and was not excited about the prospect of doing so in the next fifteen minutes. "What makes you think this woman is in mortal danger?"

"I spoke to her husband. He said she's in a bad way, unconscious, her breathing is real shallow," Mervyn responded.

"You spoke to him?"

"Yup."

"Well, I would like to talk to him myself. Can you get him on the phone?"

"Most of the lines are down. The line from Steele Swamp to Malin is down. But there is one line open, from the ranch to Alturas and back around. I'll see if the operator can patch us through."

"Who is this fellow I'm going to be speaking with and what is his wife's name?"

"Herman Vowell. His wife is Betty. Real nice folks. Salt of the earth. Do what you can, please, I've buckarooed with them and they're personal friends of mine."

While Rita completed the connection to Steele Swamp Ranch Mervyn handed the phone to Dr. Martin. Herman answered on the first ring. Dr. Martin introduced himself and said he had a few questions. "When was it that Betty began to feel ill?"

"She hides it when she's sick but I could tell she wasn't feeling well this morning. She was having some pain in her belly. My brother and I went out to feed and when we came in she was lying on the floor," said Herman.

"Was she unconscious?"

"Yes sir, she was, and she still hasn't come around. It's been a good hour."

"Is she pale or does she have a little bit of color?"

"White as a sheet. She was this morning, too, but not near as bad as now."

"Have you checked for a pulse?"

"No sir. Her heart is beating and she's breathing, but real shallow-like. She doesn't have a lot of life left in her, Doctor. She needs help real bad."

"How old is she?"

"Twenty-eight."

"Has she had any children?"

"No sir. We were hoping...."

"Could she be pregnant?"

"We were thinking she might be."

"When was her last period? Can you tell me that?"

"She missed her last two."

"Well I better have a look. I hear the plane now. I'll get a few things together. Put a pillow under her feet to elevate them. Keep her warm. I'll be there as quickly as I can."

Dr. Martin hung up the receiver. Herman had impressed him as being very level-headed, not the least bit panicky although very concerned for his wife's welfare. He had replied to each question with short, precise answers. A cool head was important. He might very well be called upon to assist. Dr. Martin had a good idea what was wrong with his new patient and he figured it was pregnancy related. He would know more when he saw her.

He grabbed his largest medical bag and went to the storeroom and took two units of army surplus dehydrated plasma and sterile water to reconstitute them from one of the foot lockers. He selected needles, a bottle of alcohol and several packages of dressing gauze. He added a can of ether and an ether mask, morphine and a few sterile items from the office. Though he knew it was not nearly enough to meet every situation he might face, it would have to do. He closed the bag and hurried out the door, stopping at the house to tell LaVon where he was going. Mervyn drove him to a 40-acre field at the edge of town where a Piper Cub was waiting.

The pilot was Bud Arnold, a thin-faced man with thick glasses. He was wearing a leather coat. He held open the passenger door and Dr. Martin climbed in and stowed his bag in the narrow space in the rear. The engine revved and even though Bud opened the throttle they moved slowly across the wet, sticky snow. It was evident they were not going to lift off before reaching the barbed wire fence on the far side of the field.

Bud eased back and maneuvered the plane to the southwest corner of the field. "If we go corner to corner we have more room." A moment later he added, "Sun's making the snow pretty sticky. We'll try packing it."

After several passes to pack the snow and several more aborted attempts to take off, it was apparent that becoming airborne under these conditions was extremely unlikely. But if they waited any longer the day would get warmer and the conditions worse. In the meantime the health of the patient was becoming more tenuous. Time was of the essence.

Bud turned to his passenger. "You're going to have to get out and push. Push as hard as you can, then jump in and hang on. The rest'll be up to me. We've got one chance. Let's make the most of it."

Dr. Martin, against all conventional wisdom, stepped from the plane into the snow. Bud revved the engine and the doctor began pushing. They picked up speed. The stench of burned fuel stung Dr. Martin's nose and wind from the spinning propeller blew icy crystals in his face. He shut his eyes and pushed as hard as he could. When his legs had difficulty keeping up with the speed of the plane he swung onto the back of one ski. As he hoisted himself toward the doorway he glanced between his legs and saw the barbed wire fence and a solid juniper post flash past below his shoes. He fell into the seat and gave a tremendous sigh of relief.

"Good job, Doc," called Bud over the noise of the engine and the rush of the wind. "We cleared by two inches, three tops."

They made a tight circle and in a few moments Malin and the symmetry of the fields, outlined by fences, was behind them. They passed over rolling hills, open country dotted by juniper trees, sagebrush and outcroppings of basalt. They flew over several herds of deer pawing to get at the grass hidden under the snow and spooked a band of wild horses that galloped away from them, lunging through the drifts.

After a short fifteen-minute flight, they came to a broad snow-covered meadow filled with cows and flashed over a barn and a house. Smoke rose straight up from the chimney. There was no wind. An improvised landing strip had been marked with gunny sacks laid end to end. Two men were adding a few last sacks near the house but they stopped when the plane roared into view.

Bud banked hard to the left and came in low, aiming for the line of gunnysacks, landing to one side of them. He cut the engine and the Piper Cub glided to a stop a hundred yards from the house. Bud called to his passenger, "Here you are, Doc."

Dr. Martin climbed from the plane and one of the two men on the ground stepped forward. "Are you the one I talked to on the phone?"

Herman nodded.

"I'm his brother, Ray," said the other man.

Dr. Martin sized them up in a glance. They looked like brothers although Herman was thin as pork rind. Ray was stockier. Ray reached for the medical bag and offered, "I'll take that." Dr. Martin gave it to him and they hurried toward the house.

Bud called after them, "I'll be up in a few minutes." He planned to turn the plane around in case the patient needed to be evacuated in a hurry.

At the house, Herman led Dr. Martin to the bedroom. Ray came in only long enough to set the medical bag near the bed and then he retreated to the kitchen where he stoked wood in the cast iron cook stove and stood there, his back to the heat. Herman soon joined him. They did not speak. There was nothing to say.

Betty lay on the bed, feet elevated with a pillow, covers tucked around her shoulders. She was unconscious, expressionless and her complexion so pale she gave the appearance of a porcelain doll. A beautiful young woman, imperiled in a place as isolated as this, caused Dr. Martin to hesitate. He felt oddly flustered but his medical instincts took over. With his stethoscope slung around his neck he opened the top two buttons of his patient's shirt and listened to the faint beat of her heart. She was fighting for her life. He instinctively knew she was bleeding internally, and that if she did not get a transfusion, and quickly, she would most certainly die.

Dr. Martin quickly mixed sterile water and plasma in a glass bottle. Holding Betty's arm he noted she was dreadfully cool to his touch. He pressed a needle into that pale skin, knowing that she had very little pressure in her veins from a substantial loss of blood and there was a very real chance he would puncture through the vein to the other side. He skillfully maneuvered the needle, hit the vein precisely and started the plasma. Within a few moments Betty began regaining consciousness. She moaned in pain.

Dr. Martin's diagnosis was a ruptured ectopic pregnancy. As he explained to Herman, it was his opinion that an embryo had implanted and developed within the tubal passageway rather than in the uterine cavity. Since the tube had relatively thin walls and little space to accommodate a growing embryo, a rupture had occurred, causing Betty to bleed internally. If he tried to transport her to the hospital she would most likely die on the way, especially considering that the small plane would not accommodate both patient and doctor. The only chance for Betty's survival was immediate surgery. But Dr. Martin was not trained to perform such a procedure by himself. He needed assistance.

"Herman, is the phone still working?" he asked.

"I think so. I'll check." Herman picked up the receiver and cranked the handle.

"Hello, Herman," spoke Rita immediately. "Did the doctor get there?"

"Yes ma'am, he's here," said Herman.

"If you've got the operator," called Dr. Martin, who had returned to the bedroom, "have her ring Dr. Tice at his office in Klamath Falls."

A few moments later Herman leaned away from the phone and shouted into the other room, "Dr. Tice is on the line."

The two doctors conferred on the diagnosis and need for

immediate surgery. "It's my opinion," Dr. Martin said, "the patient cannot survive being transported. I apologize for having to ask, but I request your assistance, Dr. Tice. As soon as we hang up I'll have the pilot in the air. By the time you reach the airport he should be landing. You can be here in an hour. Everything will be ready, but I must warn you that conditions here are rather primitive."

"Okay," agreed Dr. Tice, "I'll be there."

Bud Arnold was on his way to the house when Dr. Martin called and asked him to return to his plane and fly to the Klamath Falls airport, pick up Dr. Tice and get him back to the ranch as quickly as possible. "Betty's survival depends on how fast you can get back with Dr. Tice." It was the first time Dr. Martin had called the patient by name and somehow it made it more personal to him.

Returning to the house Dr. Martin asked Herman, "Do you have any sawhorses?"

Herman shook his head up and down. "Yes sir."

"Get them. The best light is here in the kitchen. Set them here." Dr. Martin turned his attention to Ray. "I want you to take that door off its hinges and when Herman gets back, lay the door across the top of the sawhorses. Then get a mattress and make a bed that we can use for an operating table. And when you finish that I want the fire built up and every big pan you have filled with water and brought to a boil." With that said he quickly stepped from the room and returned to check the condition of his patient.

The box springs and mattress straddling the saw horses left little space in the kitchen. The room was hot and steamy. The top of the cookstove was covered with pans filled with water. Tiny bubbles appeared near the heat source, rose and burst on the surface. Herman and Ray stood off to one side and watched Dr. Martin place instruments and towels in the boiling water. Ray turned to his brother and, though it was difficult for him, he felt compelled to speak. "Herman, if anything happens to Betty, I just want you to know; she's the finest lady in the whole world, the best wife any man could ever hope to have. She's been like a sister to me. I can't begin to tell you how much I love her...."

"I know," said Herman. Both of them had tears in their eyes.

When Dr. Martin reentered the room he took one look at the brothers and stated, "We have a lot to do and not much time to get it done. Herman, I want you to carry Betty in here and lay her on our operating table. Ray, help Herman and then get me a few more towels."

Herman lifted Betty and carried her to the kitchen. At that moment she seemed as light as a feather to him. He said a prayer under his breath, asking God to take care of her, asking God to protect her through the upcoming operation.

Dr. Martin directed Herman to help him remove Betty's clothing. Herman folded the garments and laid them in a pile on a chair. A sheet was placed over Betty. A pillow was tucked under her feet to elevate them.

Ray rushed into the room. "I think I hear the plane."

THREE

Dr. Tice had worked as a surgeon in Klamath Falls for nearly a year when Dr. Martin stopped to introduce himself. During their conversation a bond formed between the two young doctors who were both from Kansas and shared a mutual love for hunting and fishing. When Dr. Martin found himself at Steele Swamp in need of a surgeon, it was predictable that he would call for Dr. Tice.

On the way to the airport Dr. Tice stopped at Hillside Hospital to pick up a sterile surgical kit. A member of the hospital staff protested its removal from the hospital. Dr. Tice promised to have the kit returned by morning. "I have surgery scheduled at 10 a.m. and will be here well before that."

Bud Arnold was waiting at the airport. Dr. Tice transferred the surgical kit and other medical supplies to the Piper Cub. The long snowy runway provided ample room to build up speed and they lifted off easily, flying southeast across the basin country, skirting around Stukel Mountain and past the town of Malin. They flew on a straight line above the Devil's Garden to Steele Swamp, coming in low over the cattle, touching down and taxiing near the house. They were met by Herman and Ray. Without wasting time on introductions the men helped carry the equipment to the house.

Dr. Tice found the patient lying on the makeshift operating table in the kitchen, covered from the neck down with a white sheet. She was semiconscious. Dr. Martin stood beside her.

"Thanks for coming," said Dr. Martin.

"Quite an experience," replied Dr. Tice.

Dr. Martin made quick introductions, Herman first and then Ray. Each of them shook Dr. Tice's hand.

Dr. Tice took off his coat as he commented, "Plenty warm in here." He turned to Herman, "Everything will be fine. In a few weeks she will be good as new."

He rolled up his sleeves and scrubbed his hands and arms in one of the large pots of hot water. He asked Herman and Ray, who were standing near the doorway to the dining room, "You're not planning on assisting, are you?"

Herman managed to respond, "No sir. We're fine pulling a baby calf or doctoring a colt but don't figure we'd be much good to you in a situation like this."

"You should go to another room then," ordered Dr. Tice and then softening a little he added, "We'll let you know the minute the operation is complete."

The sound of Herman and Ray's hard-soled cowboy boots resounded against the floor as they walked toward the back bedroom. Bud Arnold joined them.

Dr. Tice opened the surgical kit on the kitchen counter and arranged the instruments as he would need them. From a purely medical standpoint, the objective of the upcoming procedure was very straightforward, a series of simple surgical steps: open the abdomen, stop the bleeding, remove the damaged tube, close the incision, resuscitate the patient with her own blood and additional fluids, and get her out of surgical shock as quickly as possible. The dangers were many: in her weakened state the patient might not be strong enough to survive the operation, she might go into surgical shock and never come out of it, or given the primitive conditions she might survive the operation and later succumb to an infection.

The operation began. Dr. Tice rolled back the sheet and administered a shot of Novocain in the skin of the lower abdomen. He set the syringe aside as Dr. Martin handed him the scalpel. As though he were tracing a line on paper Dr. Tice used the scalpel to make a midline incision below Betty's navel. The scalpel penetrated the skin and as he cut deeper Betty groaned and involuntarily flailed her arms and legs.

"We're going to have to supplement with ether," Dr. Tice told Dr. Martin. "I need you to assist me. Neither of those cowboys have the stomach for this, but it's been my experience that any fellow who has the guts to fly a plane will do almost anything just as long as you tell him how. See if Bud would be willing to administer anesthesia."

Dr. Martin went to the back bedroom. Coming from the hot kitchen he was struck by how cold it was back there. Herman had such an anxious look on his face that Dr. Martin reassured him with, "Everything is fine." Turning to Bud he said, "We need you."

"Sure," replied Bud. It was a relief for him to leave the quietness of the bedroom and the morose Vowell brothers. If he could help he was game for trying.

In the kitchen Dr. Martin instructed Bud how to hold and slowly drip ether onto the mask positioned over Betty's face, cautioning him to use the minimum necessary to keep her unconscious.

The reek of ether seeped from the kitchen and reached the back bedroom. Herman continued to pace. Ray sat on the bed. They both knew that the operation had begun and could only pray it would be successful.

Dr. Tice finished the incision, opened the peritoneal cavity and confirmed that the patient had indeed suffered a ruptured tubal pregnancy. Her cavity was full of blood, several hundred ccs were pooled there.

"There's the culprit," spoke Dr. Tice, as he reached toward an artery that was open and pumping blood. He clamped it, tied it off, and stopped the flow. He removed the ruptured tube, along with the tiny fetus, cleaned away the clotted blood that lay in her body cavity and salvaged a pint of blood, aspirating it with the sterile vacuum bottle he had wisely brought. The blood was put in an IV and flowed back into the patient's vein as a transfusion.

Betty was in surgical shock, her blood pressure so low she was not profusing and a unit of plasma was administered. By then the sun was sliding toward the horizon. Its reflection off the snow held the light for a while longer but as it began to fail kerosene lamps were lit. They proved inadequate and Ray was called from the bedroom to hold a flashlight so Dr. Tice could see to close the incision. Ray held the light with both hands, trying to keep the beam steady.

As soon as Dr. Tice finished he told Ray, "Let your brother know the operation went well. Tell him he can come out now and I'll talk to him."

Ray used the flashlight to walk to the bedroom where he found Herman sitting on the edge of the bed. He held the light toward the floor. Herman had his elbows on his knees and the heels of his hands covering his eyes. When he looked up Ray could tell he had been crying.

"It's over," he said. "She's doing fine. The doctor says you can come out. He wants to talk to you. I'll do chores."

The barn's familiar smells and sounds and routines, feeding the horses and the chickens, slopping the hogs, milking the cow, helped to relieve Ray's anxious mind. He was happy the operation had been successful but regretted that Betty had suffered so much. They had nearly lost her. And he was sorry his younger brother had been forced to endure the shock and the stress of it all. He knew the hardest part for Herman had been seeing Betty like that and being powerless to save her. On the way back to the house Ray turned off the flashlight and stood under the canopy of the stars and said a prayer thanking the doctors, and thanking God for sparing Betty's life.

Herman had met Betty nearly ten years earlier. He was working on the Pitchfork Ranch and his boss, W.C. Dalton, had sent him south to round up a herd of Pitchfork steers pastured on the McDermott Ranch near Morgan Hill, California. Herman was met at the train station by the McDermott Ranch manager, Johnnie Salimento, a charismatic paniolo from the Island of Hawaii. Herman was easy to spot, strikingly out of place among other travelers, with a cowboy hat on his head, a leather grip in one hand and a saddle slung over his shoulder.

As they drove away, Johnnie said, "Since I'm in town I need to drive around a while. I've got to find me a horse breaker."

"A horse breaker, huh?"

"Got in thirty head of Harry Wilson's Umbrella horses out of Nevada. Wildest bunch of mustangs I ever laid eyes on. Need to get them broke. Government's paying top dollar for cavalry remounts and if I can get them broke without a lot of investment, there's a handsome profit in it for the ranch. Had a Mexican starting them but he got throwed so many times he had bumps on top of bumps. He never even called for his wages, just headed out walking toward town. I need to replace him, if I can."

"Maybe I can help," drawled Herman.

Johnnie looked at Herman and raised an eyebrow. "I thought you were a cattleman."

"I've ridden a few broncy mustangs in my time."

"Tell you what," said Johnnie, "I'll let you have a shot as long as you don't cripple yourself for rounding up those steers."

"Give me something to do of the evenings," grinned Herman.

The following morning Herman and Johnnie began riding the mountainous terrain, rounding up every three-year-old steer wearing a Pitchfork brand. The going was rough, straight up and down, and when they finally called it quits for the day, Herman remarked, "Seventeen thousand acres and it all stands on end. That's the first time I ever wore out three horses in a single day and never lost sight of the barn."

After supper Herman met Johnnie at the corral. One of the mustangs was saddled and ready to go. "If you ride this fireball you can ride any of them."

"I'll get my own saddle."

"Naw, he's ready to go," said Johnnie. "Just cheek him and crawl aboard."

Herman had seen a man cheek a horse before; grabbing the headstall between the bit and the eyes, pulling the head around until the horse was off balance, and then clutching the saddle horn and swinging aboard. It took a powerful man to handle such a maneuver. The only time Herman had seen it done was by a broncy cowboy a long way from camp. He did not want to cheek this horse and told Johnnie so.

"Come on, that's the way it's done in these parts," chided Johnnie.

Herman pulled the horse's head around but as he shifted his weight to vault onto the saddle, the mustang threw his head and sent Herman sprawling. Herman picked himself up off the ground, dusted the parts he could easily reach and growled at Johnnie, "This time keep your nose out of it. I'll do it my way."

He caught the mustang, took the reins, grabbed a fistful of mane, and as the horse moved forward Herman used the animal's momentum to propel himself up and onto the saddle. He had been on hundreds of broncs and his feet automatically slipped into the stirrups.

In response to the bite of the steel rowels the mustang tossed his head, reared and walked on his hind legs. When this did not unseat the rider he exploded in a wild display of bucking.

Herman matched the bronc with a fury of his own. Each time they crashed to the earth, before they could go airborne again, he reached with his spurs, digging them into the horse's shoulder muscles. His wicked display of aggression was intended to show this horse and to show Johnnie, who was boss.

After more than a minute the outcome became clear. Still Herman pressed the issue. It was not until the horse had been reduced to crow hopping that Herman finally let up. The animal's last ounce of energy was drained from him and he stood in one spot, shaking like a wet dog. Only then did Herman drop the reins, throw his right leg over the cantle and gracefully slide to the ground.

Johnnie was clearly amused. "Cowboy, you shouldn't have any problem with the rest of 'em."

One afternoon as Herman and Johnnie ran another bunch of Pitchfork steers into a holding pen, Herman looked up and saw a young woman approaching on a short-coupled white horse. She seemed to flow with the movement of the horse. Herman nodded in her direction, "Who's that?"

"Betty Torrens. Her folks work here on the ranch. Her dad, Bruce, does chores and I'm sure you know her mother Leona, the cook. Great folks," said Johnnie. "Betty is a hand with horses, has patience and will stick with it until a horse picks up on what she's trying to teach it. She learned everything she knows from me. Heck of a sweet kid."

"Why haven't I seen her around?"

"Been traveling, promoting the Madrone Rodeo." Johnnie called to Betty, "Hey there."

Betty kicked her horse into an easy gallop, drew up quickly and before the dust passed her, she began flirting with Johnnie. "I've missed you."

Herman was smitten by this girl's lively emerald eyes and her engaging smile. As he took his next breath he knew this girl was for him. She seemed that perfect. A gust of wind made the leaves talk in the trees as Johnnie introduced them, "This here's

Herman Vowell. He's the buckaroo boss for the Dalton outfit, here after the Pitchfork steers, the three-year-olds anyway. This is Betty Torrens. She's my girl."

"Oh, Johnnie," said Betty. He was fifteen years older than she was and she was most certainly not his girl. She spoke to Herman. "When we moved up here I was green as green could be. Johnnie taught me to ride."

"Did a pretty dang good job of it, too," stated Johnnie with a confident nod of his head. "I'm mighty proud of her. She's the queen of the Madrone Rodeo. It's coming right up. Not something a fellow would dream of missing. Herman, you might think about laying down your entry fee. From what I've seen, you could give the locals a lesson in busting broncs."

Herman wanted to say he might just do that but found himself tongue-tied as he studied this attractive girl. He liked everything he saw. She possessed an obvious vitality that made it seem as though she must come wide awake each morning and open her arms to embrace the sun. Her tan cowboy hat was set at a jaunty angle, crowning rich brown hair that hung in curled rivulets. Light danced merrily in the emerald-colored pigment of her irises and her laughter seemed especially well suited for such a summer day. She was slender and fair, her cheeks burnished by the sun and wind. Although she was straddling a horse she did so with a refined poise, as if she had been born in the saddle. When she spoke her words tumbled forth in a breathless sort of way, as though she had just returned from galloping her horse in a big loop around the pasture. Herman felt his buckaroo heart pounding in his chest. It was so loud he was afraid she might hear it.

"Mom said to tell you supper'll be ready in a half-hour," said Betty. "I'm going for a quick ride." Turning her attention to the visitor she said, "Nice meeting you, Herman."

Herman tapped the brim of his cowboy hat with two fingers and as she touched her pony with the points of her rowels, Herman turned in the saddle and watched her ride away.

Coming from the darkness of the bedroom, Herman had to squint as he entered the kitchen. Dr. Martin and Bud had stepped outside to get a breath of fresh air. Dr. Tice was putting instruments back in the surgical kit. Betty was still lying on the kitchen door. An IV was dripping the last few ccs of plasma into her arm. The color had returned to her face and she was breathing normally. Herman felt a tremendous wave of relief sweep over him. His desperate prayers had been answered. He went directly to her, bent at the waist and kissed her forehead. She was warm to his touch and that worried Herman.

"Is she running a fever?"

"No," said Dr. Tice and he chuckled. "That wood stove puts out a lot of heat. The operation went well. It was a tubal pregnancy. An artery ruptured."

"And she's gonna be fine?"

Dr. Tice turned to face Herman. "She lost a lot of blood. It's been quite a shock to her system. It's going to take time, but I think she will recover nicely."

Herman expelled the breath he had been holding. And then he asked, "The baby?"

Dr. Tice shook his head.

Dr. Martin returned. "We can move her to your bedroom. You carry her, Herman. I'll take the IV."

Herman slid his hands beneath Betty and carried her into the bedroom, gingerly laying her on the bed. Dr. Martin hung the IV bottle on the high metal bed frame. Again Herman kissed Betty tenderly on her forehead and stepped back as Dr. Martin pulled the blankets over his patient. Speaking to Herman in a hushed tone he said, "Rest is what she needs most now."

The men returned to the kitchen. Herman and Bud removed the box springs and mattress, took down the door and set the sawhorses outside. Then Herman shook hands, first with Dr. Martin, and then Dr. Tice. He searched for the right words to express himself and settled for, "I don't know how I can ever thank you enough for coming all the way out here like you did. You saved her life. If I had lost her – well, I don't know what I would have done. Thank you."

Ray came in from chores. The men were quiet for a long moment and then Thelma Archer burst into the kitchen.

"Thelma," said Herman in surprise, "what are you doing here?"

She pulled off her gloves and extended her hands toward the warm stove. "I still can't believe the phone line didn't go down in that storm. It's a miracle."

"You rode over here?" questioned Herman in disbelief. "Through all that snow?"

Thelma nodded and replied, "That's what friends are for, Herman." As she stripped off her heavy coat she said, "Well, I don't suppose anyone has eaten. You all need some nourishment.

"Herman, Ray, go out to the cool house and cut me off a hunk of smoked ham, fetch me a couple dozen eggs, and a gallon of milk, too. I'm going to cook breakfast. I know it's not the time of day for breakfast but it's quick and easy to fix. From the looks of you, it's been a long and mighty troublesome day."

After Herman and Ray left, Thelma quizzed the doctors. "How is Betty? Did you fix her up?"

Dr. Tice explained, "We repaired the damage. She's resting comfortably and I anticipate she will make a full recovery. It will be a slow process but she won't need us. We'll be leaving soon."

Bud Arnold remarked, "It's a little on the shady side to be attempting to fly out of here. We'll have to spend the night. I can take you back to town first thing in the morning."

The distant whine of a motor distracted them. In time a military jeep, chains on all four tires, stopped in front of the ranch house. Thelma opened the door and a man tromped snow off his feet and stepped inside. Without a word he walked directly to the cook stove where he stood facing the heat. After a few minutes he introduced himself as Roland Sherman from the Forest Service office in Alturas. "I'm here to offer any assistance that might be needed."

"I believe I'll take you up on the offer," said Dr. Tice. "I promised to have this surgical kit back early in the morning and, besides, I have surgery scheduled. Would you drive me to Klamath Falls tonight?"

"You're not going anywhere," advised Thelma, "until you've had something to eat."

Roland, who had bucked four-foot snow drifts, ground his way over rocks, and jarred in and out of holes hidden by the snow, looked relieved at Thelma's announcement. He was not looking forward to the grueling return trip but starting out warm and with good food in his belly would help.

The odd collection of men sat at one of the long tables in the enclosed porch that functioned as a summertime dining room for the hay crew and the buckaroos. Thelma served them ham, eggs, biscuits and a mountain of sourdough pancakes smothered with their choice of maple syrup or strawberry preserves.

Between bites Bud mentioned, "We were mighty lucky all the way around. Until yesterday that Piper Cub had a 65-horse engine. We just switched over to a 90-horsepower engine and today was the shakedown flight." He nodded in Dr. Martin's direction. "If we had the 65, that barbed wire would have been wrapped around us like ribbon on a Christmas package."

Bud turned his attention to Dr. Tice. "Another thing, those skis are the wrong ones for the plane. And here's something else for you to think about. Before today I had never taken off or landed on snow."

"Quite interesting," commented Dr. Tice in his dry manner. "Well, let me tell you something, Bud. You were standing there with your back to that wood stove dripping ether on the mask. Did you know that ether is a very volatile substance? Any small spark can cause it to ignite. And if it had, this house, and all of us, would have been blown into northern Klamath County."

At that moment Bud found it extremely difficult to swallow.

31

FOUR

The house was quiet, except for the ticking of a mantel clock. Herman sat beside the bed, holding Betty's hand, watching her in the radiance of the moonlight. Earlier she had spoken his name and then slipped back into a peaceful sleep. He would never be able to tell her of his terrifying fear when he found her lying on the kitchen floor. His love for her was so intense that the thought he might lose her had been a physical pain, so gripping it had stolen his breath.

Herman allowed the fingers of his right hand to delicately caress her cheek and he could feel its warmth and softness, the life pulsing just below the layer of her skin. He thought to himself, as he had so often before, that he was unworthy of such a goddess. He vowed that from this day forward he would do everything he could to bring her happiness; pick her colorful bouquets of spring flowers, help her weed the garden, take her riding more often, give her anything her heart desired. He had come so dangerously close to losing her that he would never take her for granted again.

As he sat in the exhilaration of the present he remembered the past and the memories of their courtship. He was not sure exactly when he knew he loved her, maybe the moment they met, but there was no doubt of his feelings as he watched her circle the arena as queen of the Madrone rodeo. She rode her white horse. He recalled a longing, more passionate than he had ever experienced, and a fear that a saddle tramp from the Devil's Garden would never have a chance to win the heart of such a pretty girl as Betty Torrens.

Herman had entered the saddle bronc event to impress Betty. He rode to win and as he finished, 4,000 fans leaped to their feet and applauded. He stood in the arena, tipped his hat to the crowd as he searched for Betty and found her sitting on the top rail near the chutes. When their eyes met she acknowledged him and his showy ride by clasping two hands over her head in a salute.

The next day Herman's time in California came to an end and it was Betty, not his friend Johnnie, who drove him to the depot. She promised to write, they shook hands and Herman returned to the Devil's Garden and the solitude of a buckaroo's life. Several weeks passed and Herman was of the opinion that he would never hear from that pretty gal in California. But her first letter caught up with him at Weed Valley, one of the camps scattered across the Devil's Garden where the buckaroos stayed while working the cattle in that area. The mail came in with the supplies and when Herman found the letter from Betty lying on the table, his name and address written in the feminine flow of her handwriting, his knees went weak. He picked up the envelope and carried it outside, walked far enough that none of the buckaroos would bother him, and sat down on a boulder. He deliberately slit open the envelope with his pocketknife.

He savored each word he read. Betty said she was on the McDermott Ranch payroll, working part-time whenever they needed her. She said she was riding nearly every day and that the weather had been warm and that her father had a cold and that Johnnie said to say howdy. She signed it, "Your friend, Betty".

Every so often during that year one of Betty's letters would catch up to Herman and sometimes she would include a poem. Herman treasured these poems because they were windows to Betty's soul. The words revealed her emotions, observations and sentiments. It meant she trusted him. He always wrote back although it often took weeks and sometimes even months before he was in town to mail a letter. He wrote how much he had enjoyed a particular poem, answered her questions, and described how he spent his days: rounding up cattle, branding, weaning yearlings, taking steers to market, running wild horses. The letters that passed between them were informative and cordial, never romantic. They were simply two friends communicating and keeping in contact with one another.

Mr. Dalton's experiment of wintering cattle in California proved a failure. The high cost of transportation and the difficulty of gathering the wild and elusive steers from the rugged Hamilton range left the profits wandering in the hills.

The next fall Mr. Dalton sent Herman back to the McDermott Ranch with instructions to bring out every steer he could find and to shoot and butcher those that refused to be driven. Betty met Herman at the train depot in San Jose. He did not know that she had fretted and fussed about her looks before making the drive. She wore pants and a red blouse, a little makeup, just a touch of eye shadow and mascara to accent her eyes. She had clipped on a pair of small-hooped earrings, dabbed perfume behind her ears and at the base of her throat, brushed her hair, pinned it up, looked in the mirror, thought it too much, and let it back down.

The moment Herman spotted her he was amazed at how naturally beautiful she looked. He grinned, set down his saddle and grip, held his hands extended in front of him in greeting. "My, my, my, you're even prettier than I remembered."

She blushed as she took his hands. "Honestly, Herman."

"I'm being honest."

"Then, cowboy, you ought to get to town more often. That way the first girl you see wouldn't take your breath away." They laughed together.

During the drive to the ranch, their conversation soon regained the bond of familiarity they had shared the summer before. Herman watched Betty out of the corner of his eye as she drove. He remembered empty nights on the Devil's Garden, lying in his bedroll beneath the stars, dreaming about her. That ache he had carried inside his heart was gone. He felt happier than at any time in his life.

Before Herman arrived, Betty asked Johnnie if she could help ride roundup. Johnnie refused, saying the work would be too dangerous, and that he had a bad feeling something was going to happen.

"Like what?"

"I don't know what," shrugged Johnnie. "But I don't want you involved."

"Something bad?"

"Could be. Can't say for sure."

"Is something going to happen to Herman?"

Johnnie laughed. "Herman can take care of himself."

The roundup progressed smoothly. One evening Herman and Johnnie stood near the corral watching a sorrel gelding that Johnnie had recently purchased.

"He's something. That's for sure. See the way he carries himself. So much pride. Such spirit. Going to take a special man to break him." Johnnie's words could be construed as a subtle invitation for Herman to give the horse a try.

Herman watched the sorrel pace back and forth in the corral.

Breaking him would require time, knowledge and an infinite amount of patience. If Herman took Johnnie's challenge it would be because he recognized the sorrel's unique qualities. He was fast, strong, agile, intelligent and possessed a natural leader's strong heart. This horse had unlimited potential and if properly trained he could become a top cow horse. Herman pushed his hat back a few inches on his head. He nodded in the direction of the sorrel. "I might like to give it a try. If I broke him could I buy him?"

Johnnie chuckled. "Everything on this ranch is for sale. Thing is, a well-trained pony's worth a whole lot more than some wild mustang that's never been rode. But when the time comes we can talk. I'll be fair. You know that. Think you're the man to take the fire out of him?"

"It would give me a chance to relax in the evenings. Sure, I'll give it a go."

Betty often came to the corral after supper and quietly watched Herman work the sorrel. He was so intent on the training process Betty believed that if she stripped off her clothes and stood naked, Herman would not notice. His concentration made him oblivious to everything except the horse. This afforded Betty a perfect opportunity to be an invisible observer and it was immediately obvious to her that Herman was not only knowledgeable but that he had a special gift when it came to horses.

Each time the sorrel did something right Herman offered praise and encouragement. "Thatta boy. You're doing good. Stand still. There, smell my hand. I'm not going to hurt you. Let me rub your nose. Good boy. Easy. There. How does that feel?"

Herman never hurried, never made quick or jerky movements; always seemed in control, flowing from one spot to the next in long, graceful strides, every movement counting for something, every motion calculated. He was gentle, kind, firm and determined. Some trainers were heavy-handed, using a whip or a club to punish a horse; but Herman got his way by using a system of small rewards; encouraging the sorrel with a tender word, a pet or a rub, a look that said he was especially proud of a particular achievement. Herman went about his business with a self assurance that proved he was the master. The horse took notice and the accumulative effect was that, layer by calculated layer, his wild instincts were stripped away and he began to trust Herman and accept what he was teaching.

Herman moved from one step to the next. He ran the sorrel in circles, making the horse change directions with the flip of his lariat loop. When the horse allowed Herman to control his movements, he was introduced to a halter. Once broke to the halter Herman was able to lead him. After a few more sessions Herman slipped on the bridle and bit and soon had him accustomed to the blanket and ready for a saddle. It was only a matter of a few days and Herman would be riding the sorrel.

When the evening sessions ended Herman always fed and watered the horse. After that he turned his attention to Betty. They stood by the corral and made small talk, gradually drifting to the kitchen, and the desserts Leona always saved for them. They sat at the small table in the kitchen, eating and talking.

Late at night, lying in bed, Betty wondered which was her favorite time of the day. Was it when she watched Herman work the sorrel and the air seemed so thick and full of excitement? Or was it when they sat together in the kitchen and she had him all to herself? Her practical side told her that in the corral Herman showed the man he was, the consummate horseman and the gifted buckaroo. In the kitchen her romantic view was that he revealed more of the man he could become.

One Saturday Betty asked Herman and Johnnie to accompany her on a ride, enticing them with the promise of a picnic lunch. Johnnie, sensing the couple would rather be alone, thanked her for the invitation but declined. "You kids go on and have yourselves a good time."

Herman and Betty rode to a sprawling oak tree and tied their horses to a low limb. Betty spread a blanket in the shade and they sat down. From this vantage they could see across the top of the coastal hills all the way to the Pacific Ocean, stretched in a thin blue line along the horizon. They ate ham and cheese sandwiches, nibbled peanut butter cookies, drank Coca-Cola from bottles, and talked.

Betty lay back on the blanket and propped her head up with an elbow. "You've told me a lot about Ray. Do you have other brothers or sisters?"

Herman removed his hat and laid on his back beside Betty. "Three sisters. Two brothers. Faye is the oldest. Then Ina, Ray, me and Rex. Dorothy is the baby. We were all born two years apart. Ray and I were always the closest, cut from the same bolt of cloth, I'd guess."

"What kind of material would that be?"

Herman chuckled, "Certainly not silk. Something rough. Probably burlap."

Betty laughed. A bird landed in the tree and chirped a time or two before flying on. A wayward ocean breeze tickled the underbellies of the oak leaves and made them whisper.

"How about your father, what does he do?"

"He's dead."

"I'm sorry."

"That's okay. It was a long time ago. He was from Texas, cow boss for the 7F outfit. Mom has pictures; one shows him wearing a slicker and riding roundup. Cattle scattered all over those hills. The 7F must have been a big spread.

"He was working there when they got married. They came to Oregon because of Mom's sister. Aunt Emma and Uncle Frank homesteaded along the shores of lower Klamath Lake. I guess they wrote free land was available. The folks took a place next to them. That was in 1910.

"A few years later the government built a diversion dam and drained Lower Klamath Lake. All the homesteads were ruined. Turned into nothing but a dust bowl around there. So the folks moved to Klamath Falls and Dad went to driving a log wagon.

He made the run from Round Valley to the mill in Klamath Falls.

"But enough about that. I keep talking and I'll put you to sleep. Tell me something about yourself."

"Not much to tell," said Betty. "Mom, Dad, my sister Lee and I lived in a small town. The folks had a chicken ranch. It wasn't really a ranch at all, they just called it that. By the time I graduated from high school it was costing more than it brought in so the folks closed it and moved up here."

"Why did you follow? Why not get a job?"

"I came to visit. It was only going to be for a week or two, a vacation of sorts, and besides it sounded exciting, an actual cattle ranch. Until I came here, I had no idea that real cowboys existed outside of western movies. I thought they had gone out of style when the West was settled and cities sprang up."

"You're kidding?"

"No, really. I had never even considered where meat came from. When we wanted a steak we went to the butcher shop. In my mind that was where beef came from. But once we moved here I learned in a hurry. And of course I met Johnnie. He became the big brother I always wished I'd had. He taught me to ride. A person can't spend much time around Johnnie without learning to love horses as he does.

"That is pretty much the story. I'm sad to say my life is all too ordinary and colorless."

Herman took hold of her hand in his. She felt the way it warmed her. It was comfortable lying beside him on the top of this ridge holding his hand. She enjoyed the sensations and could have drifted off to peaceful sleep but she was bothered by what he had told her, that he had lost his father. She tried to imagine what it would be like if she lost her father. That would leave a terrible scar on a person's heart.

"How old were you when your dad died?"

"Five, Ray was seven."

"Can you remember him?"

"Ray remembers more than I do. Ray said that one time, when he was about six years old, he sassed Mom at breakfast and ran upstairs, locked himself in the bathroom. He waited and when he hadn't heard a sound in thirty minutes he eased open the door. There was Dad waiting for him and he jammed his foot in the door before Ray could slam it shut. That morning Dad put the fear of God into Ray and he never sassed Mom again.

"Another time a neighborhood bully knocked Ray down and rolled him around in the dirt. Ray headed home bawling like a baby. When he got there Dad told him to march back over to the neighbor's house and give that bully a whipping, or else he was going to strip off his belt and give Ray a taste of leather he would never forget. I guess Ray was more scared of Dad than the bully because he fought that kid and beat him three ways from Sunday.

"Dad liked to drink every now and again. Mom has a photo of him and he's holding a mason jar. I asked Mom what was in that jar and she said it was nothing but water. If it was water it was awfully muddy water.

"Ray tells about the time he and Dad went out of town and brought back a load of hay. They were coming up South Sixth Street with a four-horse team on the wagon and Dad stopped at a saloon, told Ray he had to go in and make a deal with a man to sell him the load of hay. He put the lines in Ray's hands and told him to wait right there and not let go. One drink led to I don't know how many but eventually Dad staggered out and Ray was still holding those lines even though his little hands were nearly frozen. Ray has always been tough like that."

"How did he die?"

Herman sat up. "Being a wagon freighter he was always out in the elements; wind, rain, snow, sleet, hail. Day after day. He came down with a cold that turned into bronchial pneumonia. Mom tried to get him to see a doctor but he could be bull-headed. I clearly remember the day they came to take him to the hospital. Two men in white coats loaded him into the back seat of a big, black touring car. The last thing he said to us was, 'I don't like this country. The minute I get out of the hospital we're going back to Texas.' But he died right there in the hospital."

Betty shifted on the blanket and laid her head on Herman's lap. She looked up at him as he gazed off toward the ocean. She liked his looks. His skin was weathered from exposure to the elements. He was lean but his shoulders were broad and his muscles had the definition of a man who worked for a living. She rubbed her thumb across the callouses on his hands. He looked down at her and smiled. She noticed faint lines were beginning to form at the corners of his dark eyes. She wanted him to talk some more. She loved the soft and fluent, almost poetic, way he strung his words together. His voice belonged on the radio.

"After he died, your mother, with six children, what did she do?"

"What could she do? She sold the wagon and horses, got enough for tickets on the train and took us back to Texas. We stayed with one side of the family for a while and then moved in with another relative on the other side. We kept doing that. Times were tough. They all had a passel of kids. After a year of living hand-to-mouth we had pretty much wore out our welcome. We headed back for Oregon and Aunt Emma and Uncle Frank.

"Took the train as far as Bakersfield. That was where our money ran out. We went to work in the cotton fields. They called me Cotton Top because my hair was so blond it was almost white and I was about the size of a cotton plant. Even the two little ones worked as best they could, dragging their sacks along. When Mother had enough money saved she bought train tickets and we went on in to Klamath Falls. We found a house to rent near Aunt Emma and Uncle Frank. Our neighbors were wonderful. They shared whatever they had with us and after a few months we were able to get a milk cow and some chickens. We sold cream and eggs. When spring came we planted a big garden and Mom canned until she was sick of it.

"Ray and I found jobs. In the morning the milk truck stopped at our house and Ray and I hopped in with the driver. Ray took one side of the street and I took the other. We carried quarts of milk to the porch of every customer and brought back the empty bottles. We did it on the run because the driver never slowed, just kept a steady pace. In the evenings we delivered the *Herald and News.* We gave Mom every cent we made but sometimes, to show her appreciation, she would give us back a nickel or a dime. I still send her money every payday, always will.

"We were poor as church mice. When the well-to-do parents bought their kids new clothes they would pass the old ones on to the Vowell family because they knew Mom couldn't afford to spend money on us. As a result we got teased about our hand-me-downs and Ray and I had more than our fair share of fistfights. Anytime there was a fight you met at the bottom of the hill after school.

"I remember going back to school after Christmas vacation and this 5th grader telling me to take off my shirt. It had been his favorite and he wanted it back. I refused and so he called me out to fight. After school we went down the hill and he said since I was only half his size he was going to give me first hit. He sucked in his belly, pointed, said to give it to him right there. I might have been young and small but I wasn't stupid. I brought one up from down around my boot tops and instead of aiming for the belly I hit him square on the tip of his chin, knocked him out colder than a wedge. After that he always made sure to avoid me. Wearing hand-me-downs like we did either made a fighter or a coward out of you. Ray and I did manage to learn how to handle ourselves."

Herman glanced at the sun, remarked, "Where has the time gone? Suppose we best be getting back."

Betty gathered up the remnants of the picnic and packed them away. As they rode off the bench Betty looked in the direction of the blue water and thought to herself how much she had enjoyed the afternoon. She had no way of knowing that, just as Johnnie had predicted, tragedy had struck at the McDermott Ranch.

Johnnie did not come in for lunch and Leona asked one of the hired men to look for him and let him know she had saved him a sandwich. A half hour later the hired man found Johnnie in the corral with the sorrel gelding Herman had been breaking. The horse was saddled, bridled and running loose with the reins dragging on the ground. Johnnie lay in the dust. The ranch hand ran to the house and hollered through the screen door to the kitchen. "Mrs. Torrens, get a doctor quick! There's been an accident."

"Who? Who got hurt?" Leona's first fear was that Betty had fallen off her horse and broken an arm.

"It's Johnnie. He's hurt real bad," cried the hired man.

Leona called for an ambulance from the town of Morgan Hill, six miles away. The road forded a creek and wound through the hills. When the ambulance arrived 30 minutes later Johnnie was still alive. They rushed him to the hospital in San Jose, but little could be done for him. He had suffered a compound skull fracture and died the next morning. It was a mystery how an expert horseman could have been killed and speculation was he had either been thrown from the horse against the concrete water trough or the horse had kicked him.

Herman took the news hard. He blamed himself for the accident. Betty took the news hardest of all. She was devastated. Johnnie was her adopted big brother. Now he was gone, gone forever. And it had happened while she was away enjoying herself. Why had she chosen this day to have a picnic? She should have insisted he go along. She felt responsible and guilty. For the longest time she could not stop crying. But as evening stretched a curtain of darkness she retreated to her room and came to terms with her sorrow by writing a poem to Johnnie. She poured her heart out to him. And when it was finished she set the paper aside and slept.

The funeral was held at St. Joseph's Church. Somber men wearing boots and cowboy hats marched up the steps. They removed their hats at the door and during the service they mindlessly fingered the brims as the priest spoke about God's eternal flame and life in the hereafter.

At the graveside ceremony Johnnie's brother told a Hawaiian legend that involved the little people and how they were the guardians of the water of life. When he finished he removed a small glass vial from his pocket and sprinkled a few drops of water on Johnnie's casket.

Betty, her parents, her older sister Lee, and Herman stood together and waited until the crowd had dispersed. With Betty clinging to Herman's arm the small group approached the casket. Though Betty had difficulty controlling her emotions she recited her poem, simply titled, "Johnnie".

> *I love these hills*
> *and their great oak trees.*
> *Every trail and spring*
> *bring back memories.*
>
> *Every horse shoe print*
> *on the dusty ground,*
> *leads me to believe*
> *that you are still around.*
>
> *If only your saddle*
> *was not so bare,*
> *if only the dust*
> *was not settled there.*
>
> *I would know in my heart*
> *you were really here then,*
> *a riding and roping*
> *I would not have to pretend.*

But each time I look
and you're not around,
I try to be thankful
For the peace you have found.

For surely you now know
your great reward,
in receiving the blessings
of our Lord.

The McDermott ranch was in turmoil without Johnnie. After breakfast the hired men sat drinking coffee when they should have been harvesting the oat hay. They took extra time at lunch and quit early because of the heat. Herman spoke with several of the men, saying he needed help rounding up the remaining Pitchfork cattle and offering them top dollar to ride, but they turned him down.

"I don't know what I'm going to do," Herman complained to Betty one evening. "Mr. Dalton said that I was not to leave any Pitchfork cattle alive on the ranch. He doesn't want to have to pay another bill for pasturing them. But I sure can't do it alone."

"I'd be glad to help," said Betty. "It'd probably do me good to get out and ride. Take my mind off Johnnie."

"Well, you do know the country." Herman was thinking out loud. "And you ride good. If you're game maybe we should give it a try."

"I'm game," said Betty and she smiled. It felt good. It seemed like ages since she had smiled.

Herman and Betty quickly discovered they worked well together. When a steer broke from the brush they were both already on the move and it seemed they always knew what the other was thinking. If one of them had the lead and tried to turn an animal the other instinctively sensed it and backed off. They were able to drive in 34 head but some refused to be driven and had to be hunted down, shot, butchered and the meat packed in to the cool room. Days spun one into another and soon only a handful of steers were unaccounted for.

Early one afternoon, on their way back to the barn to change horses, Herman and Betty crossed the hay field. The entire hay crew was standing around the stationary baler watching one fellow on the buck rake. His job was to move the piles of oat hay to the baler but his team refused to work.

Herman addressed the crew. "Somebody tell you boys to take the day off?"

"Ain't nothin' we can do unless we get hay," said one of the men.

Herman rode to the buck rake. "Looks like you're having trouble. Could I give you a hand?"

"These damn horses," the man groused.

Herman slid out of his saddle, handed the reins to Betty and told the man, "Why don't you let me give it a try."

"If I can't make 'em work, what the hell can you do with them?"

"Watch your language, there's a lady present," Herman admonished him. "What I can or can't do remains to be seen. Get off."

Herman climbed onto the seat. He told Betty to take their horses in and to relax for a while. As she moved away he spoke to the horses in a gentle voice explaining to them that they were going to be moving hay, taking it to the baler, and reminding them they had a job to accomplish. Then, picking up the lines, his tone of voice changed. It was time for work. On his command the horses moved. Herman brought in load after load and the crew sweated and pitched hay throughout the afternoon.

The replaced teamster gave up on getting his job back and walked from the field. As he gathered his gear in the bunkhouse the ranch owner walked in.

"Mr. Proctor," said the surprised teamster.

"What are you doing?" asked Proctor.

"You don't need me around here no more. You got that cowboy from Oregon thinks he can run the whole damn outfit by himself. I quit."

Proctor was a wealthy man who owned a steam ship company and lived in Oakland. The ranch was little more than a hobby for him. Johnnie Salimento had told him what a capable man Herman was; how knowledgeable he was of cattle and horses, skilled riding roundup and busting broncs, about his winning saddle bronc ride at the Madrone rodeo. Now that Johnnie was gone Proctor needed a man with proven ability to replace him.

That evening, when Herman came in with the hay crew, Proctor asked to have a word with him. They stepped around the corner of the barn and Proctor came right to the point. "I'm here today for one reason, to ask you to go to work for me. Take over what Johnnie was doing. What do you figure you'd have to have?"

"Well, sir," said Herman, removing his hat and wiping his forehead with the sleeve of his shirt. "I love this part of the country, love the people. The weather is good. I think it would be fine to work for you. But to be perfectly honest, I've got a job working as the buckaroo boss for the Pitchfork outfit. I wouldn't trade it for the world. Mr. Dalton's been good to me. He treats me like a son."

"If it's a matter of money...."

Herman held up a hand interrupting Proctor. "It's not. I'm happy where I am and that's that. But I thank you for the offer."

Herman returned home a few days later with a photograph of Betty in his pocket. She gave it to him at the train station. It was inscribed, "Herman, Forever your pal, Betty".

"Herman."

Herman had fallen asleep but he awoke with a start when Betty spoke his name. He was still holding her hand. The moon was hanging on the lip of the Cascade mountains and the bedroom was nearly dark. But he could make out the features of her face. Her eyes were open.

"Yes, darling," he said.

"I'm glad you're here, Herman." She licked her lips. They were dry.

"You're going to be all right."

"That's good," she said. There was a long moment of silence and then she asked, "The baby?"

Herman shook his head. "No."

Again there was silence. "The main thing is we have each other." Her speech was slurred. Slowly her eyelids began to close. The ticking of the clock kept a measured cadence, moments passed and Herman was left wondering if they had shared a conversation at all, or if it had been part of a dream that he had awakened from.

Every hour or so during that long night Dr. Martin left the cot that had been fixed for him and tiptoed into the bedroom to check on Betty. He thought it was touching that Herman stayed at her side, holding her hand. His patient seemed to be resting comfortably and he found no need to disturb her.

As the new day broke, Thelma started banging pots and pans in the kitchen, trying to outdo her efforts of the night before. After breakfast Bud Arnold went to his plane to warm up the engine. Herman and Ray headed to the barn and began chores. Dr. Martin checked on Betty once again and found her awake.

Dr. Martin introduced himself and asked, "And how are you feeling today, young lady?"

"Good," she said and flashed him a tight-lipped smile. "How long will it hurt?"

"You had major surgery," Dr. Martin reminded her.

"I know," said Betty. "But I was just wondering how long before I can get up? How long before I can ride again?"

Dr. Martin laughed. "Not for a little while. You need time to heal. You gave us quite a scare."

"Herman told me what happened. I can't begin to say how much I appreciate everything you did."

"You were in need of medical attention. Dr. Tice and I were able to help. That is why we became doctors. May I take a look at the incision?"

"Of course, Doctor."

Dr. Martin pulled back the covers. "That looks good. Dr. Tice did excellent work especially considering by the time he finished it was nearly dark and we were using a flashlight to see. That is going to heal nicely. You might not even have much of a scar."

Dr. Martin said that Rachel Gysbers, a registered nurse and a long-time friend of the Vowell family, would fly out and stay with Betty. He promised, "I'll come back when it's time to remove the sutures."

Betty took his hand, "Thanks again, Dr. Martin. I don't know how we can ever repay you except with our friendship."

"I am honored. I will cherish it," he replied. Betty squeezed his hand before letting go.

Herman and Ray were on the meadow feeding cattle when Herman looked up and saw Dr. Martin walking toward the plane. He waved. Dr. Martin waved back and then crawled into the Piper Cub. Bud revved the engine a time or two and began moving forward, quickly picking up speed on the crusted snow. The plane leaped into the air. Bud wiggled the wings to say goodby and flew west.

Dr. Martin was surprised to find a crowd of people waiting outside his office in Malin. Men began firing questions at him; wanting to know what the flight had been like, the extent of the surgery and details about the woman's life he had helped save.

Dr. Martin remained very matter-of-fact. "Due to an abdominal condition Dr. Tice performed emergency surgery. I assisted. The patient is 28 years old, a very pretty young woman and she is recovering nicely. This morning she was alert and talking."

"Tell us about the operation."

"The patient's husband, Herman Vowell, and his brother Ray, took a door off the hinges and using that and a couple of sawhorses they fashioned an operating table...."

It was not until this point, when the reporters took out their note pads and began writing furiously in them, that Dr. Martin came to the realization that all these men were from news agencies and that he was being interviewed. Their questions came fast. Dr. Martin answered them all and as the reporters got the information they needed for their stories they began to drift away. When he was finally alone Dr. Martin stepped inside his office and called Dr. Tice's home.

"This is Jack Martin. Is Ray there?"

"He got home about fifteen minutes ago," said his wife, Irene. "He went straight to bed. I'm supposed to wake him in an hour."

"I must have gotten back before he did. We flew out this morning."

"Ray told me the road was absolutely terrible, nearly impassible in places. He said it was rocky and they had to plow through snow drifts as tall as the tires on the jeep," said Irene. "They went clear to Alturas and then circled around. When they reached the highway they were trying to make up lost time but they hit a deer. All in all it sounded like it was quite an experience. When I wake him up I'll tell him you called."

"Please do, and be sure and mention that the patient is doing extremely well. And one more thing, Irene. Be sure and thank him for me, will you?"

"I will, Jack."

The AP carried the story on its wire service and newspapers across the country ran it. Headlines in the *Oregon Journal* stated: "Surgery In Kitchen – Ski Plane Takes Medics To Save Klamath Woman". The San Francisco *Examiner* bannered: "Surgeons Fly to Snowbound Ranch; Save Life of Woman". The Spokane *Spokesman Review* reported: "Surgeons who flew to a snow-isolated ranch house, turned a kitchen into a surgery and a door into an operating table...." And the story carried by the Santa Cruz *Sentinel-News* stated that Betty Vowell, a former resident of Santa Cruz "... is alive today only through the dramatic flights of a ski-equipped Piper Cub, successful surgery performed in her ranch kitchen, her own indomitable courage and vitality, plus a series of seemingly providential incidents...."

Dr. Martin fielded calls from relatives in Kansas and Minneapolis who had read the story. He could not believe the nationwide sensation the incident caused. It was voted one of the top ten news stories of the year.

Soon patients from throughout southern Oregon and northern California were scheduling appointments with Dr. Martin and Dr. Tice. The attention caused some jealousy in the medical community and it was suggested that the whole thing had been a publicity stunt. The staff director at Hillside Hospital called a special meeting to vote on suspending the hospital privileges of the two doctors.

The local newspaper, the Klamath Falls *Herald and News*, ran an editorial under the heading: "Medical Drama". It stated, "Not often do the dramatic incidents of the medical profession get into the papers. Doctors are peculiarly loath about publicizing their work, and only occasionally is it possible to describe publicly the things they do – as was done in the case of the kitchen operation that saved the life of a Steele Swamp woman.

"Things like that are good for the medical profession. They humanize it and dramatize it. Even in such cases, we of the newspaper find the doctors unwilling recipients of personal mention; but inasmuch as anonymous characters do not make a good story, we 'bullied' that one through in spite of the doctors' reluctance...."

That editorial seemed to placate the hospital staff and nothing more was said about the suspension.

FIVE

Bud's Piper Cub made another trip to Steele Swamp to bring Rachel Gysbers. Soon after the weather warmed, the snow melted and the ground thawed. Travel to and from the ranch became even more difficult. Calving season began and Herman and Ray were busy around the clock feeding, tending cows having calving problems and caring for sick baby calves.

Rachel stayed in the house caring for Betty. Though they had been friends for several years they had never had the luxury of being alone for an extended period of time. Rachel was a good listener. Betty told how she and Herman had come to share their life together. Rachel found herself enthralled by the love story.

When Betty talked about Johnnie Salimento's death she cried. Rachel gave her a box of tissue and waited for the story to continue. Betty dabbed at her tears and explained that after that tragedy she and her parents felt they could no longer stay at the McDermott Ranch. Her parents moved to Santa Cruz and bought a small service station. Betty moved in with her best friend from high school, Merle Bardt, and took a job as a telephone operator. During this time she continued to write to Herman.

After fall roundup in 1941 Herman telephoned Betty and mentioned he had a week coming. Betty enthusiastically invited him to Santa Cruz for a visit. "You can stay with Mom and Dad. They would love to see you, or, if you want, you can sleep on the couch at our apartment. I'm sure Merle wouldn't mind one little bit. There are a lot of fun things we can do. But I have to warn you, none of them involve horses. It'll be terrific to see you. I can hardly wait."

Herman drove south in a 1936 Chevrolet coupe he had bought with Ray. They kept it parked at the home ranch near Malin and used it to run to Klamath Falls or to a rodeo or a roping on the rare occasions when one or both of them came out of the hills from buckarooing.

Betty knew Herman would most likely arrive while she was at work. That morning she spent extra time on herself. She rose an hour early, took a long bath and chose her clothes carefully. Herman had never seen her in a skirt and, wanting to impress him, she chose a lively yellow sun dress. She slipped it on and looked at herself in the mirror. The color definitely accentuated her green eyes and brown hair. She turned this way and that. The dress fit her well and made her look feminine but the material dipped low in front and revealed a little too much. Eventually Betty decided to choose a more conservative dress, a blue one with white lace and buttons running up the front. It was not as eye-catching as the yellow but Betty thought it suggested a feminine quality without shouting it. She slipped her feet into a pair of low-heeled sandals and hurried off to work.

Merle arrived home at the apartment before Betty. Herman recognized the tall blonde from Betty's letters and caught up to her as she opened the door. He introduced himself and she invited him into the small apartment. She offered him a drink and they sat on opposite ends of the sofa and visited while they waited for Betty.

Betty and Merle had known each other since first grade. They were very different from each other. Merle was likely to say whatever popped into her head. She could be flighty and insensible, silly and a little coarse, especially when she drank. Merle liked alcohol. Betty was dead set against it. But in spite of their differences they had remained best friends.

Merle was drinking a beer and Herman a soda when Betty came home. Herman set the drink aside and stood. With youthful exuberance Betty ran to him and flung herself into his arms.

"You're certainly a sight for sore eyes," she exclaimed. "How long have you been here?"

"A while."

Betty glanced in Merle's direction. "And how are the two of you getting along?"

"Famously," said Merle.

"Let's go to dinner and then maybe we can catch a show. How about it, Merle, want to come?" asked Betty.

"Naw, run along. Have fun."

After the movie Herman asked Betty if she wanted to drive around for a while rather than go directly back to the apartment.

"That would be fine with me."

They drove along a winding road that brought them to a hill overlooking the beach. Herman stopped the car and turned off the engine. Betty giggled.

"What's so funny?" asked Herman self-consciously.

"Have you ever dated in this town before?"

"No. Absolutely not."

"Well, then," said Betty, with a bit of good-natured mocking to her tone of voice, "I would like to know how you happened to find this place. This is lovers lane."

"It is?"

Betty scooted across the seat, next to Herman. She could tell that he was embarrassed and it amused her. She said, "The kids come here to park and neck. Is that what you had in mind, Herman?"

She took his hand then and kissed it, turning it over, palm up, individually kissing each of his hard-earned calluses. Continuing to hold his hand she looked at him and waited. And waited. Waited some more. And finally she twisted around in the seat and turned into him. He had no choice but to hold her in his arms and then, at last, he kissed her.

That kiss was like releasing all the water held behind a floodgate. The emotions poured out and he cradled her and rocked gently back and forth as he spoke to her in a voice barely above a whisper, telling her, "We've known each other a long time now. We've written letters back and forth. We've become good friends. You probably don't know this but you should. I've been in love with you since I first laid eyes on you."

She sat up abruptly and pulled away. "You're telling me this now?"

"Reckon so." Herman was dreadfully afraid he had made a mistake, that his feelings were not mutual, that he had overstepped his bounds and from this moment forward their relationship was doomed. He might have even destroyed their friendship. He had been too honest, said too much.

She melted into him. "Tell me again."

"The whole thing?"

"Just tell me you love me."

The words came easily. "Betty, I do love you." They kissed again and there was unbridled passion in their kiss. And when they separated Herman saw tears on Betty's cheeks and ever so tenderly he kissed them away, one by one.

"You can't imagine how many times I've prayed that you would tell me that. How many times I wanted to tell you, to write those words to you in a letter, to shout them from the top of a mountain. Herman, I love you."

They spent a long time parked there. Eventually he drove

back to her apartment, kissed her goodnight and drove to her parents' house to spend the night. Considering what had transpired they both felt that was the right thing for him to do.

The following day they rode bikes on the boardwalk and frolicked in the surf. They played like a couple of kids. That evening they skipped the movie and drove directly to lovers lane. There, in that romantic setting, with the moonlight glinting off the Pacific and the incoming tide pushing white waves against the sandy shore, Herman again told Betty he loved her. And then he surprised her by asking, "Will you marry me?"

She laughed and cuddled against him, said yes she would marry him. It was as perfect as any moment would ever be. A gust of wind gently rocked the car. The roar of the surf seemed far away. Betty whispered, "I love you so much. I want to spend my whole life with you."

He was holding her in his arms when she began to giggle. She pulled away and with an obvious display of theatrics she announced, "We have to leave, right now. Drive me home. Mother is just going to die. And Mister, if you want to marry me you have to be a gentleman and ask Daddy for my hand. You have to."

When they reached the Torrens's home Betty leapt from the car and sprinted to the door. She dashed inside and pulled her mother into the kitchen to tell her the wonderful news while Herman went to the front room to speak to her father.

"Bruce, I have something I need to discuss with you," said Herman as he uncomfortably shifted his weight from one foot to the other. Bruce stopped in the middle of filling his pipe with tobacco and laid it in the ashtray.

"What is it?" he said.

"I proposed to Betty tonight and she said she would marry me. Is that all right with you?"

Bruce retrieved his pipe. He finished filling it and then he lit the tobacco. He smoked and contemplated. It seemed as though he took an almost sadistic delight in tormenting Herman. Finally he blew out a cloud of smoke. "That's okay by me but her mother might have a different opinion. You better check with her."

When Herman stepped into the kitchen Leona was dabbing at her tears with a tissue and for a fleeting instant Herman wondered if they were tears of despair.

"What is wrong with you, Mister?" Leona scolded, and then she laughed. "My little girl thinks the world of you and it takes this long for you to finally get around to asking her to marry you?" She hugged him. "Gee, Herman, I'm so glad you're going to be part of our family."

The following day was Sunday, December 7, 1941. Herman and Betty returned to the beach. It was a warm morning with just a slight bit of wind blowing in from off the ocean. Sea gulls hung on the breeze, waves gently slapped the shore and Herman and Betty built a sand castle, waded in the ocean and lay together on the sand. They held hands. They kissed. They talked about their future together.

The idyllic morning was shattered when a man came running down from the parking lot hollering, "They just bombed Pearl Harbor! The Japs bombed Pearl Harbor!"

Herman and Betty looked into each other's eyes, searching, knowing from that moment forward their lives would never be the same. How could something like this happen, especially now? Would they still be able to marry and have a life together? So many questions were contained within the lingering look they exchanged. There were no answers. They stared off to the west, to where 3,000 miles away a war had erupted, a war that had reached all the way across the Pacific to touch their lives.

Betty cried. "Will you have to go?"

"I don't know. Probably so."

In the months ahead Herman and Betty continued to correspond. From the tone of her letters it was evident that Betty wanted to get married as soon as possible. Herman wanted to get married, too, but he was expecting to be drafted into the military and was unsure what the future held, and so he stalled.

In August 1942 Betty sent a telegram to Herman. It was routed to the telephone operator in Alturas. She called Steele Swamp and read the message to Ollie Stratton, the wife of Jerry Stratton, ranch manager. Ollie neatly printed each word on a piece of lined paper. "TO HERMAN VOWELL STOP ARRIVING IN KLAMATH FALLS 4:00 AM AUGUST 11 STOP WE WILL GET MARRIED AUGUST 12 STOP CAN HARDLY WAIT TO SEE YOU STOP I LOVE YOU STOP BETTY."

Ollie was so taken aback by the message that she had to lower her squat frame onto the nearest chair. Girls most certainly did not propose to men. They did not take matters of that magnitude into their own hands. Ollie was absolutely appalled by the gall of this girl. And then the reality of the situation began to sink in; given the war, would Herman ever have made the commitment on his own? Would there have been a convenient time to tear himself away from the cattle and his job as buckaroo boss and marry this girl, take her on a proper honeymoon? Never. Ollie had to chuckle. This girl Betty had an incredible amount of spunk. Ollie admired spunk.

A dozen thoughts raced through Ollie's mind. Today was August 10. She knew Herman was at the Weed Valley buckaroo camp because Jerry had taken them supplies only two days before. If Jerry were not away chasing cattle he could run the telegram out to Herman, but Ollie knew he would not be in until after dark and by then it would be too late. Ollie would have to drive to Weed Valley herself and deliver the message to Herman. It pleased her to think she was going to have a hand in such a romantic adventure.

She followed the Hackamore Road, not much of a road at all, to Mowitz and then turned off onto a dim trail that wound through the sagebrush and bypassed the largest boulders. She reached the cabin at Weed Valley, set the telegram on the table and wrote a note to Herman. The note was simple and to the point. "This came for you today. In case you don't know, today is August 10, tomorrow will be August 11." She signed it and figured that was about all she could do. But she was disappointed. She had wanted to see Herman's face when he read the telegram. She knew his face would flush ten shades of red.

One of the other buckaroos was the first to find the note and read the telegram. As soon as Herman came in the note was shoved under his nose and one of the men announced, "Why don't we ride to Steele Swamp and take my Model-A. It'd save riding 30 extra miles. Besides, you've gotta have a bachelor party and you can't have one without us."

With only a bit of daylight remaining the men quickly saddled fresh mounts and rode to Steele Swamp. When they reached the ranch they hurriedly swapped their horses for the Model-A pickup. Herman made a point of swinging by the house and thanking Ollie and then they drove to Malin.

There were two bars in town and the men walked from one establishment to the other, noticeably louder and drunker each time they crossed the street. Herman followed along but he only sipped sodas. As a boy he had once shared a jug of muscatel wine with a couple friends and had been sick for three days. He vowed he would never take another drink of alcohol. The men respected him for his self-discipline, but that did not keep them from drinking.

A few hours after the party ended Herman packed a duffel with a change of clothes and left the men sprawled on the beds in the bunkhouse. He drove to the train station in Klamath Falls, arriving a few minutes before the train pulled in. Betty was wide awake and full of enthusiasm. Herman was surprised to see Merle Bardt with her.

"I didn't want to travel alone, besides Merle is going to be our witness," offered Betty.

Betty had it in her mind she wanted to be married on her mother's birthday, August 12. There was no time to waste and as soon as Herman rounded up the luggage from the baggage cart they started south for Reno.

Herman drove through the day with Betty snuggled against him. Merle wrapped herself in a blanket and slept against the door. Eventually, when Herman became too tired to drive, he pulled over and slept for a few hours. They continued on and when they reached Reno they rented a single motel room. Herman spent the night on a roll-away and the girls slept in the bed.

In the morning Herman asked Betty, "Where do you want to get married?"

Betty replied, "Not in one of those tacky wedding chapels where they stamp out marriages like cookies. I want to get married in a church."

"A particular one?"

"Any church is fine by me."

"Mom is a lifelong Baptist. It would please her if we got married there," said Herman.

Herman drove to the First Baptist Church where he asked the minister if he would marry them. The minister looked at Herman with a pretty girl on each arm and asked, "Have you made up your mind which young lady you wish to marry, or do you plan to wed them both?"

"One's probably plenty. How do I decide, eeny-meeny-miny-mo." Herman draped an arm around Betty. "I choose this one."

"Before I marry a couple I require them to attend a marriage class."

"But we don't have time," protested Betty.

"It so happens class begins in a half-hour. I can marry you after that," said the minister.

The ceremony was a simple affair with Merle and the minister's wife acting as witnesses. When it was over the bride and groom, and Merle, got back in the car and drove straight through to Santa Cruz. They left Merle at the apartment and went to Bruce and Leona's house where they spent their wedding night.

The following day they packed Betty's belongings into the Chevy. It was loaded to overflowing with personal items, Betty's entire wardrobe, and everything Leona thought they might need to live on a cattle ranch. Bruce and Leona stood on the sidewalk as Herman and Betty drove off. Leona exclaimed, "Goodness sakes, ya' all look like Okies on the move."

At the Oakland city limits, traffic increased and driving in such conditions made Herman nervous. Betty remarked that she was familiar with the streets and comfortable driving in heavy traffic. Herman pulled over and told her to take the wheel.

The sun was shining, traffic had thinned and Betty was cruising along without a care in the world when a motorcycle policeman appeared alongside, motioning her to the side of the road.

"Oh-oh," remarked Betty and Herman, who had been catching a cat nap, came awake.

"What is it?"

"I'm being pulled over, and look, I'm only doing 45. I don't know why he's stopping me. Would you get my driver's license, Honey? In my purse, there on the floor."

As Betty searched for a safe place to pull off the road Herman retrieved the license. He gave it a cursory glance and told Betty, "Your license is expired."

"Can't be."

"It expired two months ago."

"What'll we do?"

"Only one thing we can. Let's make a run for it," kidded Herman and then he told her, "Maybe he won't notice."

The motorcycle officer approached the car and asked Betty, "Young lady, do you know how fast you were going?"

"Yes officer," said Betty politely. She flashed him her prettiest smile. "When you motioned me I looked at my speedometer and I was only going 45."

"Could I see your license, please." Betty handed it to him.

He continued, "Well, Miss Torrens...."

Betty interrupted, "I'm Mrs. Vowell now. We just got married." She reached over and patted Herman's knee.

"Congratulations," said the officer. "Mrs. Vowell, you obviously didn't realize, but you're in a 25 mile per hour zone. A little ways back you passed a sign, a sign big as a barn, stating that fact." He bent at the waist and took a gander at all the clothes and things piled in the back seat. He told her, "If I were to write you a ticket it'd cost you more than your entire honeymoon trip. So, go on. Have yourselves a happy life, and oh, one thing more, if I were you, from now on I'd pay a little more attention to highway signs." He handed back the license, returned to his motorcycle and pulled into traffic.

When he was gone Betty tucked the license back in her purse and told Herman, "Maybe you better drive. He didn't give me a ticket and he didn't notice my license was expired. I'm afraid I've used up all my luck."

The remainder of the trip was uneventful. Betty nuzzled against Herman and even slept for a few hours with her head resting on his shoulder. They reached Alturas and turned onto the dirt road leading into the Devil's Garden. Betty was fascinated with the scenery. They passed through fifteen miles of hills covered with ponderosa pine and then broke onto a high plateau of sagebrush and junipers with scattered lava rock and rocky outcroppings to provide points of reference. From Herman's letters she knew this was the Devil's Garden, a big country where a cow could eat her way across seventy miles, from Malin, Oregon to Alturas, California and never come up against a drift fence.

"Look over there," said Herman, pointing to a band of horses standing off to the north side of the road. Their ears were perked and they intently watched the passing automobile. "Wild horses."

"Oh, stop, please."

Herman stopped and shut off the motor. A warm breeze

blew toward them from the west and it carried the sweet smells of earth and sagebrush. The stallion, a black horse with a long gray mane and tail, took a few tentative steps toward them. He tested the wind and when he could smell nothing he tossed his head and whinnied. A sorrel mare moved up to stand with the stallion but he drove her back with the others.

"How beautiful," said Betty, enthralled by the sight and the romance of it all. "Isn't he magnificent?"

"He is."

"Will you get me a horse like that?" Betty hugged Herman's arm.

"I'll get you ten like that," said Herman. He turned the key and pressed the starter. As it whined and the engine caught, the stallion whirled, reared in the air and drove his little band of mares off into a ravine and out of sight.

The road forked, one way led to the ranch at Steele Swamp and the other to the camp at Weed Valley. Herman suggested he take Betty to Steele Swamp, saying the cabin at Weed Valley left a lot to be desired.

"You want to take me to Steele Swamp and dump me?" asked Betty. "Is that what you have planned?"

"Figured you'd be more comfortable there. We only have a couple more days at Weed Valley and then we'll be working out of the Swamp for a month."

"I married you. I'll go where you go."

Herman knew there was no point in arguing. "All right, young lady. Weed Valley it is."

The road deteriorated to little more than a trail. Here and there tracks in the dust proved another automobile had passed that way. Herman pointed them out, explaining Ollie Stratton had driven all that way to deliver Betty's message.

"It seems like a hundred years ago that I came in and the boys handed me your telegram. So much has happened in just a couple days," said Herman.

Betty pulled herself up and tried to give Herman a kiss on the cheek but just then they hit a rock and the car bounced and swayed. She was thrown off course and wound up giving his nose a glancing smooch. They were still laughing about that when four cowboys appeared and rode directly to the car. Herman did not stop. He knew they would tease him and he kept driving.

"It's the old married man," greeted one of the riders.

Another offered, "Howdy, boss. How's married life treating you?"

The third rider rode alongside the passenger's window, which was down, leaned over in the saddle and politely said, "Howdy, Mrs. Vowell, welcome to Weed Valley."

The fourth rider stopped in the middle of the trail and it was obvious he was not going to budge. Herman had no choice but to stop. The rider called to Herman, "'Bout time you got here."

Herman and Betty exited the Chevy and Herman made introductions. "This is my wife Betty. Betty, this is Norman, Smoky, Les, and that's Jim."

Each of the cowboys politely tipped his hat and stated how pleased he was to make Betty's acquaintance. And then Herman addressed the men. "Don't you boys have work to do? We'll visit when you come in."

The cowboys returned to working cattle and Herman drove to the small cabin at Weed Valley. It was located on a rise that overlooked a broad meadow of lush grass. Herman killed the engine. He opened the door and after he climbed out he held it open as Betty scooted past the steering wheel and put her feet on the ground. Herman was stretching from the long drive and had his arms raised in the air. Betty took hold of his belt and drew him to her. She wrapped him in an embrace. "It's just like you described, only more beautiful than words."

Herman pointed out a rock that overlooked the meadow and said, "I sat right there and read your letter, the first one you ever sent. Not even in my wildest dreams could I have foreseen that, one day, you and I would be married and standing here." He kissed her then. They were still kissing when the cowboys came galloping into view. They rode directly to the cabin and in a quick flurry of activity removed their bedrolls and pitched tents a discreet distance away.

"What are they doing?" asked Betty

"I think they're giving us the honeymoon suite," said Herman. Betty blushed.

The following morning Herman took Betty on a ride to the north end of the valley where high on the slope sat the skeleton of a two-story house. Herman told Betty how a man named Buchanan had once owned Weed Valley and that he had built the house overlooking his holdings as a monument to himself. He brought in a sawmill, skidded logs to the site and milled the giant timbers. He spared no expense and even imported hardwood from back east for the floors. The house was complete except for the windows and doors when Buchanan dropped dead. The grand house was never finished. The heirs divided the holdings and sold Weed Valley to Mr. Huffman, a prominent Alturas rancher. Later, when his residence on the SX Ranch burned to the ground, Mr. Huffman had the Buchanan mansion dismantled, including the hardwood floors, and transported to his ranch headquarters. He rebuilt his home and had enough lumber left over to build a barn.

With the story concluded Betty shook her head. "It's hard to believe that all of one man's grand dreams have been reduced to this. It looks like the bleached bones of a dead whale washed up on shore. Someday I'm going to come back here and write a poem about lost dreams."

They spent three days in Weed Valley and for Betty it was a heavenly time. The men cut out the gentlest horses from their strings and gave them to her to ride. She rode beside Herman as they worked the cattle and she drank in the beauty of this big, new country she now called home. The only thing she did not do was cook. When the men gathered for supper she apologized to them. "I'm sorry. My mom is a good cook but I never learned. If you show me how I catch on quick."

"You're just lucky you can ride," Smoky told her dryly.

Norman teased her. "They say the quickest way to a man's heart is through his stomach. How did you ever catch Herman?"

"As soon as I saw her, she had my heart," said Herman. "Now why don't you teach her how to make biscuits."

On the third day the cattle were driven to the meadow at Steele Swamp. Betty rode with the men and after they put the cattle on pasture, Herman and Betty rode back to Weed Valley and brought out the car, tying their horses to the back bumper and driving slow. When they reached the house at Steele Swamp Herman introduced Betty to Jerry and Ollie.

Ollie gushed, "I'm so glad everything worked out for you kids."

"As I understand it I'd probably still be waiting at the train station if you hadn't delivered my telegram to Herman," said Betty. "Thank you, Ollie."

"Think nothing of it," said Ollie and then lowering her voice so only Betty could hear she asked, "How would you like a hot bath?"

"Absolutely love it," sighed Betty.

"Come along," directed Ollie and then turning to Jerry she said, "Hon, show Herman their bedroom. You can help him carry things in."

After her bath Betty did what she could to help Ollie in the kitchen and when it was time to eat, Ollie rang the triangle loud and clear and the hay crew and the buckaroos came in and sat at two long tables set up in an enclosed porch. The buckaroos sat together at one table and the hay crews at the other. The buckaroos were a proud bunch and it would have been beneath their dignity to sit with the simple men of the hay crew.

Betty helped Ollie serve steaks, mashed potatoes and gravy, biscuits, churned butter, corn on the cob and peas fresh out of the garden. For dessert they served apple cobbler with whipped cream ladled on top. The men were hungry. They ate with only the bare necessities of conversation, usually to grunt a request to have something passed to them. Betty was astounded at the quantity of food they consumed. The men at the McDermott Ranch never ate like these men.

While Ollie and Betty washed dishes Ray came in. He had been at Wildhorse camp for the past three weeks but word had been sent from the home ranch that Herman had run off to Reno to get married. Ray walked directly behind Betty, took off his cowboy hat and said to her back, "I'm Ray, Herman's brother."

Betty raised her hands out of the dishwater and turned around. Even though her hands were dripping wet and trailing soap suds Ray took her right hand and shook it in a gentlemanly fashion. He was beaming at her.

"My gosh," said Betty and then recovering a little, she added her own enthusiasm to the shaking of hands and said, "I sure am glad to finally meet you. Herman has told me so much about you. It seems as though I must have known you for years and years."

"I ain't near as bad as he makes out."

"Oh no, he's only told me good things," said Betty with a wink.

"Are we talking about the same guy, Herman Vowell?"

"That's him." Betty dried her hands and hugged Ray. Bashful Ray didn't quite know what to do, didn't know if he should hug her back or not. He just stood there feeling foolish and awkward.

"Sit down," said Betty, "visit with us while we finish up."

"I just rode in. I need to tend my horse."

"You can sit for a while."

"All right, for a minute."

Ray had little to add to the conversation. Mostly he nodded his head and said "yep" or "ah-huh" or "that's right". His personality reminded Betty of something Johnnie once said, that the best horsemen are quiet, steady and, above all else, blessed with unflagging patience. She remembered a time Johnnie was training a horse that kept throwing his head. Betty called out, "Why don't you make him stop that?" Johnnie replied with a calm, even tone to his voice. "I will, but not all at once."

It seemed to Betty that Ray held all the special qualities of a true horseman, just as Johnnie had described them. He also had that quiet confidence in himself, the same as Johnnie and Herman possessed. In some ways Ray reminded her of Johnnie and in others he was more like his brother. That was not quite right, she concluded. All three of them were alike in more ways than they were different. Give or take a little here or there, they could have been the same man.

That night, when Herman and Betty adjourned to their bedroom, Betty playfully told Herman, "It was great meeting your brother. I really enjoy him. You're lucky. If I had met Ray first the two of us might have run off and gotten married." She started to sit on the bed to pull off her boots but Herman stopped her.

"Don't sit there," cautioned Herman. He got down on all fours and peered under the bed. "Just as I thought," he said. He reached in his pocket, produced his pocketknife and with mock pleasure proceeded to cut the string that fastened a cowbell to the bedsprings. He also severed a length of twine that ran from the cowbell, across the far corner of the room and out the window that was slightly ajar. Holding the clapper he showed the bell to Betty, grumbling, "That Jerry Stratton and those no-good buckaroos."

Betty did not understand. Herman told her, "Don't you see? As soon as we got settled in bed those son-of-a-guns were going to ring this bell. Guess I showed them. There'll be no chivaree tonight." And then he laughed.

In the morning Herman was up before daylight. He leaned on the bed and told Betty, "Take the day off my sweet little sugar cake. Stay around here. Get acquainted with the place."

"I want to help," protested Betty. "I want to ride."

"Not today. We've got some tough country to go through and we won't be back until after dark. You're entitled to a day off every once in a while. Go back to sleep, darling."

"Be careful."

They kissed and Herman moved away. Betty lay in bed and listened to his footfalls, the door shut and silence rushed in. She slept, awoke once and heard Ollie in the kitchen but fell asleep again. When she finally woke it was nearly 8 o'clock. She dressed and put on an extra layer of lipstick. Her lips were already chapped from the combination of wind, sun and the dry high desert air. She found Ollie weeding the garden, a fenced half-acre just west of the house. To the south was a bunkhouse, several sets of corrals, a big barn and numerous outbuildings. Towering poplar trees, planted in a row, provided shade to the southeast. A small lawn surrounded the house and here and there were patches of colorful flowers. Trees in the orchard were heavy with plump, red apples. To the west was the loveliest view of all, Steele Swamp. Haying was almost finished and stacks of loose hay, looking like giant loaves of brown bread, were scattered randomly on the thousand acres of green meadow.

Early that afternoon the crew finished haying and to celebrate the occasion Ollie, with Betty's help, prepared a big dinner of fried chicken and all the trimmings. For dessert Jerry churned ice cream.

Thelma Archer dropped by to introduce herself. She explained to Betty that she was the nearest neighbor to Steele Swamp. Her husband Ernie managed the Willow Creek Ranch. She confided to Betty that she cooked only out of necessity, that her real love was to be out in the hills on horseback, buckarooing with the men. Betty felt an immediate kinship with this woman and told her, "I know exactly what you mean."

By the time the sun went down Thelma had returned home and the hay crew had gone to town to get drunk. The following morning Betty rose with Herman and spent the day riding roundup with the buckaroos. For the next month she helped gather cattle off the surrounding country and drove them to Steele Swamp. She had never known such freedom and joy. Being with Herman night and day made her love him all the more.

One evening in September Ollie confided to Betty that Jerry had bought a small ranch in Surprise Valley and that they would be moving soon. The chores of cooking and keeping house fell to Betty. By then the buckaroos had moved to the home ranch so there was only Herman and one hired man to cook for and Betty did not mind. Once her chores were completed she still had plenty of time to ride and help work cattle.

A few weeks after the Strattons moved, Mr. Dalton drove his dark-green Ford pickup to Steele Swamp. He liked to have a new pickup every other year but with the war going on he thought he should do his part and hang on to this pickup a while longer than normal. He slowed as he approached the house. Betty saw him and was concerned he might stop. She stepped away from the window. It was not that she was afraid of Mr. Dalton, they had met once when Herman took her to the home ranch; it was simply that she felt uncomfortable in his presence. He was an imposing man, owner of one of the largest ranches in the West, wealthy, and made no bones about the fact he was boss of the outfit.

William Carr Dalton had first come to the Pitchfork Ranch in 1900 at the request of his uncle, Jesse Carr, a California rancher who laid claim to thousands of acres of rangeland along the California-Oregon border. Jesse Carr filed for the Pitchfork Brand in 1874 and in an effort to delineate the boundaries of his empire he hired hundreds of Chinese laborers to construct a rock wall. It became known as the "Wall of China" and surrounded 80,000 acres. As settlers arrived and filed on legal homesteads they dismantled the wall where it crossed their property. But because of the ruggedness of the country Carr was able to maintain his holdings in the Devil's Garden.

Within a few months of his arrival the young man was made ranch manager and when Jesse died in 1912 W.C. Dalton became a principal owner. The holdings included the home ranch, Dry Lake, Steele Swamp and several hundred thousand acres of range leased from the government.

Those who had business dealings with W.C. found him to be stern and serious, but always trustworthy, honest and fair. He was a man of his word and his handshake was his bond. Behind his back some men referred to him as the "Old Man" or "Old Man Dalton", others called him Bill or W.C. but Herman and Ray had utmost respect for the man and never called him anything but "Mr. Dalton".

Mr. Dalton continued past the house to the corral and parked. He strolled to the fence and stood there surveying the meadow. It made him proud to see all those fat, bred cows. In a few months they would begin dropping their calves. That was his favorite time of year. To him looking out over a field and seeing the baby calves was like watching dividends on an investment grow and mature.

For a long time Mr. Dalton gazed at his cattle. He was lost in quiet contemplation but at last he came to a decision and, giving a tug at the brim of his cowboy hat, he set off in the direction of the barn.

Herman was mucking an alleyway, shoveling manure into a spreader. When the side door opened, a shaft of light caught his attention and he looked in that direction, instantly recognizing the bulky shadow with the sunlight to his back as Mr. Dalton.

"Herman, you in here?"

"Yes sir, Mr. Dalton." Herman leaned on the handle of the manure fork and waited. He had worked for Mr. Dalton for six years. Mr. Dalton had taken a chance on Herman, hiring him as buckaroo boss before he was ready for the job, allowing him to grow into the position as he learned about cattle and the Devil's Garden country. And now Herman had it in the back of his mind that with the Strattons gone, Mr. Dalton just might offer him the job as ranch manager at Steele Swamp. It made a lot of sense. Since he was now a married man it would be difficult for him to continue his old ways, moving from one cow camp to the next without any one place to call home. Steele Swamp would be the ideal situation. He and Betty had even discussed it as a possibility.

As Mr. Dalton drew near he handed out a rare compliment. "Well, Herman, the cows look nice and fat. And the steers weighed in at more than they ever have. I sent most of them out last week."

"Good year for grass," offered Herman. "That rain in July really helped green up the country."

"Yes it did."

Never one for unnecessary conversation Mr. Dalton stood in silence and Herman allowed him the indulgence. Mr. Dalton liked to talk about cattle and about history but he savored silence, and that was why he enjoyed riding with Herman and Ray. The Vowell brothers never had to fill up the quiet with mindless chatter as so many other men felt compelled to do. If you were quiet you could hear the birds, the wind whispering through the juniper and sage, the rhythmic clopping of the horse's hooves on the hard packed volcanic soil, the creaking of the saddle leather. That day in the barn the quiet stretched until Mr. Dalton finally chose to speak.

"Herman, I don't have anybody to run Steele Swamp. I was wondering if you and Betty would like to take over; feed this winter and calve out in the spring. It would surely help me out if you would accept."

"I'd really enjoy that, Mr. Dalton. But the one you'd have to okay it with is Betty."

"Why don't you go get her, Herman. Bring her out and I'll ask her."

When Herman walked into the kitchen with a grin on his face Betty knew exactly what he was about to tell her. She bubbled with excitement, "What did he say?"

"He wants to ask you something."

"Me?"

"Yep," drawled Herman.

"I know what it is. He wants to know if we'll spend the winter here. Tell him yes!"

"He wants to hear it from you," said Herman taking her by

the arm and propelling her toward the door.

Betty pulled away, untying the apron as she headed toward the bathroom. "I need to brush my hair and put on a dab of lipstick. It'll just take a second."

Herman and Betty walked outside together. Mr. Dalton had come out of the barn and was standing beside his pickup. He waited until the couple reached him before he spoke.

"Hello, Betty," he said, and getting right to the point he asked her, "I came out to see if you and Herman would be interested in spending the winter at Steele Swamp. Come spring if I like what you've done and you like it here we can make it permanent. What do you think, Betty?"

"I think yes."

"Then the job is yours," said Mr. Dalton. He turned to Herman, extended his hand and said, "You're my new ranch manager and if it's all right with you I'm going to ask Ray to be buckaroo boss."

"That would be great," sputtered Herman. "Just great."

With his business concluded Mr. Dalton opened the door of his pickup, slid behind the wheel and just before he started the engine he cranked down the window, leaned through the opening and told Betty, "You need to get your grocery list together. Everything you might need to hold you over for three, four, sometimes five months. In this country you never know. I've seen a big storm blow through in early November. All it takes is one big storm and you're snowbound until spring."

Herman and Betty stood and watched Mr. Dalton drive away. Betty put an arm around Herman's waist. She smiled. "This is a dream come true."

Rachel had been attentively listening to Betty and she was sure she had never heard a more romantic story. She told Betty, "I know you love Herman and he loves you. I think the strength of that love brought you through the operation. It gave you the will to live."

"Our love and this slice of heaven on earth where we live. I wouldn't want to give any of this up."

SIX

Thanksgiving 1942, Herman and Betty's first year together at Steele Swamp, was a festive occasion. Herman's mother Myrtle came to visit and stayed for a week. She and Betty talked for hours and became good friends. Betty wanted to know everything; how Myrtle had managed to keep the family together after her husband died, how she had dealt with the loneliness and isolation of losing a husband, and all the details about Herman and Ray growing up.

Myrtle confided she used to tell Herman and Ray stories about their father. But it reached the point where she regretted having said anything because those stories only seemed to further arouse their desire to become cowboys. She shrugged and told Betty she didn't suppose it mattered a single iota what she had said, that those two boys were going to do whatever it was they were going to do. And since forever, just like their father, all they wanted was to be cowboys.

One day Betty said to Myrtle, "You've never mentioned how you met Art. What was it like the first time you laid eyes on him? Did you know he was the one?"

Myrtle smiled at the memory. "First time I saw Art was when he and another cowboy came to the house and asked Daddy if they could take my sister and me to a dance. Art was bigger than most cowboys; six feet tall and a few pounds shy of two hundred. Handsome as all get out, he was. I never did ask how he happened to see us or know where we lived, but anyways, Daddy said we could go to the dance, but only if we rode in a buggy. I think he figured two buckaroos would never be able to come up with a buggy. But they did – a buggy with a green team." She laughed. "My sister and I barely took our seats when those horses ran off. We had ourselves a real donnybrook, a genuine runaway. I was scared as the dickens and yet at the same time it was reckless and exciting. Back then Art was a drifter, roaming wherever the wind blew him. But we fell in love and he gave up his wild ways.

"Art, he used to have a bit of a temper. One time we were traveling in a wagon from Klamath Falls to the homestead. It had a canvas cover. A group of men standing on a street corner made fun of our outfit. One hollered and asked if we were looking for the Oregon Trail, or some such thing. Art told the team to whoa, tied his lines off on the brake, got down, walked over to the men and grabbed the biggest fellow by the nose. He marched him over to the wagon and made him apologize to me.

"On occasion he did enjoy the spirits. When he drank, his playful side rose to the surface." Again she laughed. "He could be a real prankster. But not all his jokes went over well. Like the time I was in the outhouse and he roped it. I couldn't open the door. He started rockin' it back and forth with his horse, pretty near tipped it over. Now it's kind of funny, thinking back on it, but when it happened I wasn't the least bit amused. But Art seemed to be enjoying himself. He laughed like a crazy man and that made me all the more angry."

The memories brought out something which Myrtle normally kept hidden deep within her soul. When she talked about Art there was a gleam in her eyes and Betty knew that after all the years, all the trials and tribulations, she still loved that man with her whole heart. Because of that undying love she had never wanted another. Betty could appreciate that kind of love, that unwavering devotion and single-minded commitment to another. That was exactly how she felt about Herman.

One night in January 1943, when the earth had been hammered into silence by a thick layer of snow and all the animals were curled in sleep, Betty nestled against Herman on the couch, a blanket wrapped around both of them. She thought back to her conversations with Myrtle and asked Herman when he first realized he wanted to be a cowboy.

"Well golly," said Herman, "that goes back a long way. Ever since we were knee high to a grasshopper, Ray and I wanted to be cowboys. We used to hike up to the livery stable in Klamath Falls, there on South Sixth Street just off Main. We'd rub the horses down as they came in, feed them hay and grain, muck manure out of the stalls, generally help out around the place. The livery man couldn't afford to pay us since business was slow on account of most folks were switching over to automobiles. Once in a blue moon he'd slip us a nickel or a dime.

"We lived for horses. When we weren't messing with them we'd climb into the loft and lay there, smelling the hay and the horses, dreaming of being horseback, pushing a herd of cattle across the open range. Whenever a wagon or a traveler riding a saddle horse passed the house, Ray and I'd tag along behind until either our legs gave out or the sun went down. We were positively crazy about horses.

"Every Monday Mother gave each of us a quarter for lunch money. That was supposed to last all week. But Ray and I went without eating. We saved our money and when we had six dollars we visited the saddle shop on Klamath Avenue. Ray held onto the money. I did the talking. We wanted the saddle maker to build us a bridle.

"He wanted to know what we were gonna do with a bridle. I said we were aimin' to catch a wild horse and break him. He nodded like maybe he had been a buckaroo in his younger days and still had a hankering for that life. I suppose from the way we were dressed, in worn clothes that didn't fit properly, he figured we'd never be able to afford a horse even if we somehow managed to get one for free. But he wasn't about to spoil our dream.

"He said he supposed he could build us something and wanted to know what kind of a budget we had to work with. Ray opened his hand, held out the six dollars to show him. He asked how long it had taken to save that much. When I said three or four months that impressed him and he suggested we ought to start with a grazer bit and, to keep the cost within reason, he offered to cut down some busted driving lines he had lying around and make us a head stall and reins. He said to come back in a week and he'd have it ready.

"That was about the longest week of our lives. Come Friday, just as soon as we got out of school, we ran to the saddle shop. We were so proud of that bridle we took turns carrying it, but when we reached home Mother threw a hissy fit, said we scarcely had food for the table and certainly not enough to squander on a bridle. She wanted to know how we had paid for it. I told her we saved up from our lunch money.

"Mother was pretty clear about things. She said she gave us money so we could eat. Eating well was important. And we most certainly did not need a bridle because we didn't even own a horse.

"Ray told her we were fixin' to get ourselves one. She said no, we were not getting a horse. She ordered us to march right back down there and ask the saddle maker to give our money back. No amount of logic, pleading or tears could convince her otherwise.

We got the money and gave every last cent to Mother."

The month of January was marked by a series of storms. Betty told Herman she did not care how cold it got because they had their love to keep them warm.

One evening, as they were washing the dishes from supper, Betty asked Herman to tell her about his first buckaroo job. The story was too long to tell in one setting so Herman spread it out over several cold winter evenings. Each time he came to a logical stopping point he would tell Betty, "To be continued," and take her hand and lead her to the bedroom.

Herman said his first real paying job on a ranch came in 1933. He was 17 and Ray was 19. A.W. Schaupp, an attorney and a neighbor, arranged for the two boys to spend the summer living and working on his ranch, 20 miles from Klamath Falls in the west end of Poe Valley. Vaughn Woolever, a cowboy from Miles City, Montana, was ranch foreman. He took Herman and Ray under his wing and taught them about ranch life; how to tend chores, take care of a horse, ride and rope.

Every Sunday morning Vaughn allowed the boys to stage a rodeo and try to ride the milk cows. There were fifteen cows and one by one the Vowell boys led them into the corral and tied them to the snubbing post. They tossed a rope around the cow's middle and either Herman or Ray, depending on whose turn it was, would jump onto the cow's back, grab hold of the rope and holler to be turned loose.

Neither of them could ride the cow they called Zebra Dun. In their minds she was elevated to mythical status as the rankest and wildest bucking cow in existence. One Sunday Ray managed to ride Zebra Dun. He leaped to the ground and whooped. Vaughn came on the run to see what the commotion was about and Ray bragged he had finally ridden Zebra Dun. Herman confirmed it.

"If you rode her once you ought to be able to ride her again," said Vaughn, nodding in the direction of the seemingly docile cow. "Show me."

Ray crawled back on Zebra Dun and she tossed him so high he completed one full somersault and a little more, landing on his back and knocking the wind out of himself.

"I don't believe you ever rode her," snorted Vaughn as he walked away.

The only horse Vaughn allowed Herman and Ray to ride was an old mare he kept around the place as a pet. She was fat, gentle and slow. Herman and Ray constantly hounded Vaughn to let them put a flank cinch on one of the saddle horses and try to ride it.

"I don't want my ranch horses bucked out," Vaughn told them. "It puts funny ideas in their heads. Next thing you know I'm working cattle and out of the clear blue I've got a rodeo on my hands. Naw, I don't want my horses picking up bad habits."

At harvest time the neighbors worked together, going from one field to the next, cutting hay and putting it up. When they came to the Schaupp Ranch the work teams were brought to the barn at noon, watered, grained and allowed to rest. Herman and Ray ate dinner quickly and started for the barn.

"Leave them horses alone," Vaughn called, but the boys kept going without acknowledging they had heard him. When Vaughn and the other men came out to the barn they found Herman sitting astride one of the work horses.

"I told you these horses need their rest. Now get down," ordered Vaughn.

"Would if I could," said Herman sheepishly. "Every time I so much as flinch he goes to bucking and it's all I can do to not get throwed."

Vaughn took hold of the horse's halter and as Herman slid off Vaughn told him, "If I ever catch you pulling such a stunt again I'll whip you within an inch of your life." But Vaughn was smiling when he said it. He saw a lot of himself in the Vowell brothers. When he was younger he was constantly pitting himself against the wildest bucking broncs he could find. Then he fell in love with a girl, got married and became a father. They had two young daughters and Vaughn could no longer risk injuring himself. If he could not work there would be no food on the table. And, he concluded, he did not heal as quickly as when he was twenty and in his prime. Though he could not ride rough string any more, he took a vicarious thrill watching Herman and Ray test themselves.

Ray invested every dollar of his first paycheck on a little bay mare with white legs and a stripe on her face. She was four years old and had never been ridden. He called her Queen. The first time he tried to ride Queen she bucked him off. The second time she bucked him off. Before attempting to ride Queen the third time, Ray led her to a recently plowed field. He figured at worst the landing would be a little softer and at best the soft soil would tire Queen and he could make the ride. His logic proved sound and before long Queen gentled down and accepted Ray's weight.

Ray rode Queen and Herman rode a gentle saddle horse that belonged to the ranch to the 4th of July rodeo in Klamath Falls. When they reached the rodeo grounds Ray overheard the stock contractor complain that he was short on stock and sure wished he could get his hands on some good bucking horses. Ray rode Queen close to where the man was standing and offered, "If you want, you can buck this mare of mine."

The contractor glanced at the size of the horse and remarked, "I may be desperate, but not that desperate."

"She's bucked Ray off nine times and me three times," added Herman.

"I've seen that horse," said a nearby cowboy. "She gets right with it, bucks real strong like and stays after it."

"I'd be the laughing stock of Klamath County," groused the contractor. He walked away. But as the saddle bronc event was set to get underway he looked Ray up. "If I wanted to try your little mare what would it cost me?"

"Five dollars," said Ray. "If she don't buck you owe me nothin'."

"Fair enough. Pull your saddle and run her into the chute."

The cowboy who drew Queen, a Klamath Indian who weighed at least 250 pounds, looked as if he would surely overpower the small mare. But he lasted three jumps and was unceremoniously thrown in the dirt. He lay there for a long time before several cowboys went into the arena and pulled him to his feet.

The following day six men were advanced to the finals. The contractor found Ray again, "I have five good horses. You want to buck your horse again? I'll pay you ten."

"Suits me."

The cowboy who drew Queen complained. "I come all the way from Texas and draw a kid's pony. This'll be too easy. It ain't fair."

Of the six riders in the finals, five made their ride. The only one who bucked off was the Texan. Afterward he stood dumbfounded while Ray threw his saddle on Queen and rode her away.

By the end of that summer Herman had bought a small, green-broke mare, half-sister to Ray's Queen. She was a pretty bay with a bald face, four white stockings and a light colored spot on one side that made her look almost like a pinto. Herman called her Joker.

Herman and Ray looked for work that fall but times were tough and jobs scarce. They picked up odd jobs where they found them.

In March 1934 Uncle Frank, who was leasing farm ground near Tulelake, took Herman on a drive to look over his fields. On the way back he asked if Herman would be interested in farming.

Herman told him that he wanted to work on a ranch. "I'd like to find a job where I could ride every day and work cattle."

Frank pulled to the side of the road, took off his hat, wiped a sleeve across the moisture on his forehead. "Sure I couldn't interest you in farming?"

"No sir. I want to be a cowboy."

"In that case we ought to make a run over and see a friend of mine, Leo Donavan, see if he needs any help." Frank pulled onto the road and drove about a mile before turning down a lane leading to a house and barn. They passed a sign that read, "Corpening & Donavan Cattle Company".

Frank said, "They run a thousand head. Might just be in need of an extra hand."

As they approached the barn Herman spotted a black Chevy coupe. A man was reaching through one of the windows to extract a hen. He held her to his stomach as he turned toward the approaching automobile. Frank drove within a few feet of the man and stopped. He got out. Herman followed.

The man continued to hold the chicken, petting it, gently moving a finger over the head and down the neck, following the lay of the feathers.

"How you doing, Leo?" said Frank. "Looks like you caught a live one."

"Window won't roll up and she has it in her mind to nest on my back seat," explained Leo. "If I don't get her back to the hen house she lays her eggs right here. I'm afraid she might go to settin', and if she does I'll be afoot."

Uncle Frank laughed, then introduced Herman to Leo Donavan. "Herman thinks he wants to be a cowboy."

Herman picked up on the conversation. "I was wondering, Mr. Donavan, if you might be in need of any help with your cattle."

"So happens, I could use a man. We're moving 300 yearlings from headquarters to spring pasture on the Meiss Ranch. Sixty-six miles. Four-day drive. You interested?"

"Yes sir, I certainly am," said Herman with real enthusiasm, although he was a bit disbelieving that a man petting a chicken was about to hire him for his first buckarooing job.

"Have a horse?"

"Horse, and saddle, too."

"Be here the day after tomorrow."

"Yes, sir."

"Drive starts early morning. Bring your bedroll. We'll take care of the grub."

"Thank you, sir." Herman wanted to shake Leo's hand but Leo turned away and, without another word, walked toward the hen house. Frank opened the car door and climbed behind the wheel. Herman got in and as they started to drive forward he asked, "I don't want to jeopardize my job but I was wondering if maybe Mr. Donavan could use Ray, too?"

Frank chuckled to himself, engaged the clutch and stepped on the brake. He said, "Only one way to know, better go ask."

Leo Donavan had opened the door to the hen house and turned the hen loose inside. She flapped her wings and dipped down to take a dust bath. He watched.

"Mr. Donavan."

Leo turned. "Change your mind?"

"Not at all. I'll be here. But I was just wondering – I got a brother, two years older than me, and he's got his own horse and saddle and would love to ride and drive cattle. Suppose he could help out?"

"Bring him along," said Leo. It was at that moment the hen took the opportunity to squeeze between Leo's legs. She went running for the black coupe, Leo in pursuit.

After telling the family his wonderful news Herman discovered his mother was none too happy to think that her two boys were going off to buckaroo. She had hoped they would find a trade, or at least an honorable profession to follow. Uncle Frank helped to smooth it over. "The boys have their minds set on being cowboys. Corpening & Donavan is one of the best cattle ranches around. They couldn't start with a better outfit."

It was 35 miles to the Corpening & Donavan ranch. The first day Herman and Ray rode as far as the Schaupp ranch. Vaughn, who was saddling his horse, smiled at them as they rode in. Even before they dismounted Herman blurted out that he and his brother had been hired to drive cattle to the Meiss Ranch for

Corpening & Donavan.

"Congratulations," Vaughn said. "You're going to be passing through some mighty rough country. Your horses shod?" Herman and Ray shook their heads. "They need to be. Your horses have pretty small feet, probably ought or double ought. I don't believe I have any shoes that would fit but you're more than welcome to go through the pile of used shoes there on the south side of the barn. You should be able to locate something and make do with it. The hammer and nails are there by the anvil."

"We never shod a horse before," said Herman.

"You've watched me," said Vaughn. "Better get to work while you still have daylight." He swung onto his horse and rode toward the upper valley.

"How are we supposed to find the right shoe," Herman asked Ray. "And then fit it to the foot?"

"First things first," said Ray. "We need to trim them and then we'll see what we have."

They started with Queen because she was the gentlest of the two saddle horses. Ray worked on her feet with a shoeing knife, taking up one hoof at a time and cleaning down to the frog. He pared what he could from the overgrowth of the hooves and cut the remaining excess with long-handled nippers, gripping the handles and squeezing them with both hands, rocking the tool back and forth to gain leverage. He worked his way around the perimeter of each hoof. Finally he evened and flattened the bottom and around the edge of each hoof with a rasp.

It was dry and dusty that spring and as Ray worked, Herman happened to notice Queen's prints in the dirt. He told Ray he had an idea. When Ray was finished, Herman led Queen to the south side of the barn. He made note of the tracks she left in the dirt and then dug in the pile of used horseshoes until he found one that appeared to be the right size. He laid it over one of the tracks and then went to the anvil and used the hammer to slightly change the curve of the shoe, standing the heel of the shoe against the corner of anvil and striking the hammer against the shoe's toe. Once. Twice. Three times. The noise of metal against metal sang loudly. He took the altered shoe back to compare it to the track and pounded it on the anvil some more, until the shoe fit the track perfectly. Then he moved to the next hoof print.

When they had four shoes matched to the tracks Ray set out to attach the shoes to Queen's feet. He took up a small hammer from the shoeing box, tucked a half-dozen shoeing nails in the corner of his mouth as he had seen Vaughn do, and curled under one of Queen's front feet. He fit the shoe to the hoof and drove a nail through the toe of the shoe and into the hoof. He gripped the exposed nail end in the hammer's claw and worked the claw back and forth until the nail snapped off. He worked his way around the shoe. During this process, if Queen were to shy and jerk her leg free, the exposed nails would have cut through Ray's hand or the inside of his thigh. But Queen, except to lean her weight on Ray, was the perfect subject. Ray gripped the pastern more tightly between his knees and finished sinking the last nail.

Herman took a file from the shoeing box and handed it to Ray. He cut a small groove into the glossy outside of the hoof near each nail. Next Herman handed him a block of iron and Ray used it to pound the broken ends of the nails into the groove and clinch them over.

When he finished Ray unceremoniously dropped the foot and groaned as he straightened. Beads of sweat dripped off his nose. He draped one arm over Queen and took a blow. "One down, seven to go."

Vaughn returned as they were putting the last shoe on Joker. He asked if they had had any trouble. And even though their sweat-soaked shirts told a different story, the boys said the shoeing had gone about like they figured it would.

Vaughn inspected their work. "Not bad for your first time. Tell me, boys, how did you have sense enough to turn the bevel the right way so the nail comes out instead of going into the quick?"

"We didn't know there was a right and wrong way," said Herman.

"Guess you were just lucky," said Vaughn.

Herman and Ray ate supper with Vaughn and his family and shortly afterward went to bed, tired but looking forward to the following day with eager anticipation.

In the morning they helped Vaughn do chores, ate breakfast and then headed south at a leisurely pace toward the headquarters of Corpening & Donavan. Leo Donavan met them at the barn as they rode in. "You boys store your saddles over there in the tack room. Turn out in that corral."

He nodded in the direction of a man unsaddling a horse a short distance away. He was red-faced and had thick features strikingly similar to Leo's. But this man, who was a good six to eight years older than Ray, had a wide sprawl of a nose humped and flattened from multiple breaks. "That's Ed, my little brother," Leo said. "Best horseman around. Never seen a horse he can't ride. Been around cattle all his life. If you pay attention he can teach you a lot."

"Ed, these here are the fellas I was tellin' ya about, Herman and Ray Vowell. They're gonna help us move cattle. Show 'em the ropes, if ya will."

Herman and Ray pulled their saddles and turned their horses loose with the other horses in the corral. Free of the saddles, Queen and Joker found a good spot and rolled. Ray threw in an armload of oat hay but Ed told him, "You ain't feedin' a flock of chickens. With oat hay a horse will only eat the heads and leave the rest. Give 'em double what you normally would."

Ed was not sure what to make of the two new hands his brother had hired. They were young and small and scrawny. The way they rode in – on horses not much bigger than ponies, one of them carrying a blanket tied on back of his horse that had unrolled and was dragging in the dirt – did not illicit much confidence in their abilities. He recognized them for what they were, green kids with a hankering to be cowboys.

Leo went on about his work, leaving Ed with Herman and Ray. The three of them stood in silence, watching the dozen or so horses move about the corral. New shoes struck sparks on small rocks. The air smelled of horse sweat, the musty scent from the nearby marsh and the bitter sweet tang of sage. The whinnying and nickering of the horses establishing their ranking in the herd curled over the trio as they eyed each individual horse and quietly made note of which ones they felt capable of running across the rugged scab flats and rifts and slants of the hills they would cross.

"What's your pick?" Ed asked Herman. The sudden question caught Herman off guard but he had already made his choice and pointed out a raw and sturdy horse with a good attitude, a horse that would be willing to deliver a day's work. Ed nodded in agreement. "No doubt, he's the best of the lot. Now, in my opinion, the meanest horse out there would be that bay gelding. Think you could ride him, Herman?" He pointed, "The big one over there. That one."

"Reckon so."

"There's enough daylight to find out. Grab your saddle. I'll run him into the round corral."

Herman swung onto the horse and the big bay rose into the air and crashed to earth. He twisted and grunted and screamed his frustrations. When the horse had spent himself he stood quivering. Herman tickled him with his spurs and the bay stepped out and worked in circles, one way and then the other. When Herman was satisfied he pulled the horse to a stop and slid to the ground.

Ed was impressed. He thought he just might be able to make bona fide cowboys out of these young men. He pointed out the bunkhouse. "Get yourself situated. Bell rings in 'bout a half-hour. Bring your appetite. One more thing, the men in there are farmers, hired on for planting. You're buckaroos. The worst buckaroo is a thousand times better than the best farmer. Remember that. So don't put up with any guff from those sod busters."

The inside of the bunkhouse was one long, narrow room with beds down either side. A wood stove and a hand pump with a basin under the spout sat near the middle. The floor boards were rough-cut pine, solid lumber spiked to joists as thick as a man's fist, fitted together to form a floor worn smooth by years of scuffling boot leather. Between the boards were thin cracks silted tight with a slurry of dust, manure and sand. Noticeable depressions were worn from the door to the hand pump and on to the stove, and from the stove to several of the bunks. The interior walls and ceiling were made of tongue-and-groove pine lumber painted over with a thin layer of whitewash. Near the stove, the wall and ceiling were a dingy gray from smoky residue. Several men sat on their bunks, talking and smoking cigarettes but they stopped when Herman and Ray entered. They followed the new hires with their eyes. With one blanket to share between them, sleeping together made the most sense to the brothers and they chose the double bed at the far end of the room and sat down, leaning their forearms on their knees. The quiet stretched as the two groups stared at each other. Before long the farmers picked up their conversation where it had been interrupted.

The loudest of the bunch was an old man still wearing his work gloves. Herman gently elbowed Ray. "Bet he wears those gloves to bed." They chuckled quietly and watched the man who buttoned his stained work shirt to his throat and probably bathed once or twice a year. He had an expansive memory of himself that contradicted this stage of his life, where his body was in the process of shrinking away from his hands, head and feet. He was telling stories about what a randy son of a gun he used to be. At one point he gestured toward Herman and Ray's end of the room. "It'd take two boys like that just to carry my water for the day." Herman wondered if they were going to have trouble with this shriveled old man but then the bell rang and the men disappeared in the direction of the dining hall.

Herman and Ray followed the farming crew. Ed was already there and introduced the new buckaroos to Mrs. Corpening, calling her Aunt Nonie. The cook brought in a platter of thick steaks and handed it to Ed, who speared a steak onto his plate and handed the platter to Herman who passed it to Ray. Next came mashed potatoes and a bowl of brown gravy, followed by a bowl of carrots and another of peas. The buckaroos were always served first. The food was good and there was plenty of it.

After supper Herman and Ray walked to the bunkhouse, and in the dim light at their end of the room they settled themselves under the single blanket. One of the men blew out the lamp and the room was dark and silent until someone popped a wooden match head into flame with a thumbnail and smoked the last cigarette of the day. When he finished he stabbed out the butt in a glass ashtray. It clattered. He spit a flake of tobacco on the floor and lay back with a contented groan. The crickets came alive and a great horned owl hooted. Men coughed, sputtered, wheezed and snored. Herman and Ray blocked out the odd assortment of strange sounds and slept.

They awoke to a cold, dark room. Footfalls at the far end followed one of the men who lit a lantern and then moved on and built a fire. Several men rolled out of bed and lit cigarettes. One by one the men went to the hand pump, worked the handle up and down and splashed their faces with the cold water. Before long the bell rang and everyone moved through the dark toward the dining hall. As the men passed the coffee pot they poured themselves a cup. Herman and Ray did the same. They had never tasted coffee and when Herman took a sip he was jolted at the bitter taste. He saw one of the other men sweeten his coffee with sugar and thought he would give it a try. He ladled in two spoonfuls and thought that was better.

After breakfast they saddled the horses. Ed and Ray rode off to one field to gather cattle while Herman and Leo pushed a herd from another field. At one point a yearling doubled back on them and Leo told Herman to go after it. Herman coaxed Joker into action and when the yearling tried to sneak past him, Joker dropped low, wheeled around and brought the yearling through the gate on the run.

"You're riding a pretty fair horse there, sonny," Leo told Herman.

"Thanks," responded Herman.

The cattle were gathered into a herd and, though they bellowed and protested being pushed from their familiar feeding ground, they lined out and allowed themselves to be driven. Around midday clouds began massing over the mountains and marching east. Temperatures tumbled, a stiff breeze came up and occasionally the dark underbellies of the clouds spit snow at them. By late afternoon they reached the holding pasture at the Haskins place. While the yearlings were secured behind the barbed wire enclosure the man who drove the chuck wagon, loaded with food, bedrolls, and hay and grain for the horses, started a fire and put on a pot of coffee. That fire attracted the four buckaroos and they stood near it warming themselves and sipping hot coffee while they waited for supper.

By the time they finished eating it was near dark. Leo unrolled his bedroll near the fire. Ed suggested to Herman and Ray, "I'm going to sleep in that wagon over yonder. With one blanket to share, the two of you are in for a long night. You're apt to freeze. Might as well bunk with me."

The wagon was old and one of the wheels was broken, which caused it to cant at an odd angle. Ed said, "I'll take high side." Herman and Ray crawled in the box and pulled the wool blanket over themselves. They fell asleep quickly but in the middle of the night Ray, who was on the low side, felt as though he was being squashed and moved to the high side, as did Herman shortly after. Come morning, when Ed awoke and looked around, he wanted to know, "How did I get on the bottom?"

In spite of the cold that had crept into their bones Herman and Ray had to laugh. And they were still amused when Ed told the story to Leo while they were gathered at the campfire eating breakfast. That day they pushed the cattle twenty miles and held them over at a pasture below Sheepy Ridge. Herman went to Leo and asked, "Mind if Ray and I ride over yonder?"

"Why would you want to do that? Haven't you got in enough riding today?"

"Those old buildings, that's our old homestead. We were born there," explained Herman. "We want to have a look around."

"Have at it," said Leo.

Herman and Ray rode to the site. The house was small and square as a box with a lean-to built on. Boards were coming loose and curling. Not a pane of glass remained and the vacant windows looked like dark expressionless eyes. When Herman cautiously stepped onto the porch the planks groaned and sagged underfoot while dust leaped up in small explosions with each footfall. He peered inside. It was impossible for him to imagine that anyone had ever lived there. The sun came out for an instant and then retreated behind a cloud and as the light grew dimmer the dirt and cobwebs seemed to come to life, rising off the floor or falling from the ceiling into the empty space that the retreating light had abandoned. Herman backed away.

On the back side of the house, where the Vowells had dumped their trash in a shallow pit, Ray found a pair of cowboy boots that he remembered. They had fancy red uppers with white stitching. The bottoms were worn through. It was obvious they had received plenty of use. Ray held them up. "I got these one Christmas. Gee, I really loved these old boots." With the clarity of a glass negative he saw that Christmas morning and was lost in memories until a gust of cold wind brought him back to the present. He set the boots on the ground, side-by-side, as if it were Christmas morning all over again and a boy's feet would soon slide into the top grain leather and bring them to life. He turned away, leaving the boots on that isolated patch of alkali ground.

As they walked toward their horses Ray said, "I kinda wish we could take those boots with us."

Herman swung onto the bed of an old buckboard and sat there cross-legged. The horses were near enough he could hear their careful steps, the pull and snap of a few early grass stems as they grazed. He took solace in the familiar sounds. "You can't hold onto your childhood with a pair of old boots."

"It's not that, it's just I hate leaving them out here to fall completely apart," responded Ray.

For a moment there was no wind. The storm had passed but there were still a few lingering clouds and off to the west the sky was pumpkin colored. Herman could feel the anguish of his family having lost the land and the memories of having lived here were as keen-edged as knap-sharpened obsidian. There was a pain to it he chose not to explore. He stepped to the ground. He would ride away, put some distance between himself and this place he had once called home.

As he mounted he said, "Ray, you know what today is?"

"Yeah, 21st of March. The day Dad died. Been 13 years now." They rode in silence. Color seeped from the day and gray shadows marched across the landscape. As they neared the campfire Herman said, "Fate brought us here today. I wonder why." Ray offered nothing and Herman let it go at that.

The following day they made Archie West's place at Red Rock and on the fourth day reached the Meiss Ranch near Macdoel, California where they turned the yearlings onto pasture. With the drive completed Herman and Ray were afraid they were without a job but Leo told them, "If you boys don't have anything waiting for you I'd like you to stay on and help bring over the cows and calves. You up to it?"

"Sure enough, Mr. Donavan," said Herman.

"You bet," said Ray in agreement.

The second drive, pushing six hundred head of cows and calves, was slower going but it seemed that spring had finally arrived in the basin. The days were marked with brilliant sunshine and the afternoons were warm, although at night the temperature dipped below freezing and in the morning there was frost on the grass.

Because this drive took six days instead of four, one night the cattle had to be held in the open. Leo explained they would take turns riding herd. "Ed, you and Herman ride first shift. Ray and I will spell you at midnight. Ride easy. Don't do anything to rile up those cows. And boys, for godsake, don't sing. I ain't in the mood for a stampede."

There was no moon and the night was pitch black except for the stars that glittered like live embers. Leo and Ray took over at midnight. They rode in opposite directions around the herd. At one point Leo struck a match to check the time on his pocket watch. It was then he thought he heard his name being called from the far side of the herd. Slowly he circled, allowing his horse to find the way, until he heard Ray say, "Is that you, Leo?"

"Yep."

"I think Queen stepped in some wire," said Ray. "Could you have a look see."

Leo got down from his horse and moved toward the sound of Ray's voice. He reached in his pocket, brought out a wooden match and struck it. The tiny puddle of light in the blackness of the universe illuminated the horse and rider. Queen's hind feet were badly tangled in a ball of twisted barbed wire. Leo said, "Don't know why we didn't see a hazard like that in the daylight. Not a thing we can do, not 'til morning. Even if we had a lantern I'd be hesitant to try. Better just wait. If she goes to moving she'll only get wrapped up worse, probably panic, likely kill herself. If she does, you get away from her. Try and keep her quiet. Sit tight. Come morning we'll cut her loose."

Ray and Queen stood like a granite statue of a horse and rider. The cold crept in and after five excruciatingly long hours, the Milky Way began to dim and the morning star appeared and twinkled brightly. The sky along the eastern lip came alive with a blush of amber that progressed in intensity and changed color to a delicate salmon pink and then orange and finally a burnished rosy red. Ed used a pair of wire cutters to free Queen from the tangle of wire. When she was free she moved away with tentative steps. Ray tried to dismount, managing to throw his right leg over the cantle but when his feet hit the ground his legs buckled and he went down on all fours. His cold muscles would not support his weight. Herman and Ed came to his rescue. Ray wrapped his arms around their shoulders and allowed them to carry him to the fire.

After the second drive was completed Leo said, "I'd sure like to keep you boys on the payroll but this here depression has taken a strong hold on everyone. Come roundup time I could use you but I don't have anything to keep you busy through the summer."

Herman and Ray found work buckarooing here and there, a day or two at a time. When buckarooing jobs became scarce they took a big step down, working on the ground as simple farmhands, moving on when the job was finished.

Ray resorted to farming on shares in Poe Valley. At harvest, the price of grain was so low that Ray had nothing to show for his summer's work. Herman took a job working at Laird Landing Ranch.

Fred Westfall, who seemed much older than his fifty-odd years, lived on the ranch. He rode when there was need for him and on those occasions he would strap on a pair of plain brown chaps. The brand of every outfit he had ever worked for was burned into the leather, brands overlapping brands. Ray joined Herman and Fred at Laird Landing to feed cattle during the cold weather months.

One day after breakfast Fred said to Herman and Ray, "There's a lot of horses 'round these parts just runnin' the hills. Farmers gone broke in this here depression, left the farm an' their horses; town folks bought 'emselves cars and don't wanna fool with horses no more. Once a horse runs wild ain't nobody owns 'em. Why don't ya round 'em up, buck 'em out. Be somethin' ta do. Better'n just killin' time, 'sides ya might be able ta sell 'em once they're broke an' make a little extra spendin' money."

Rounding up wild horses gave Herman and Ray something

to do after feeding. They gathered the horses in the hills, held them in makeshift corrals, broke them to halter and trained them to lead. They trailed them to Laird Landing where Herman and Ray took turns bucking them. That was the payoff, that was fun. If they sold a horse they figured it was icing on the cake.

Those winter nights in the bunkhouse Fred spun stories about the days he had spent buckarooing in Nevada. He said every ranch in Nevada was at least 100,000 acres in size and the cowboy was king. He said when his job with Clyde Laird ended he was taking off, returning to the wide-open spaces of the Silver State.

"As soon as the grass comes on an' the cattle can be turned out, the two of you are gonna be lookin' fer work," he told them. "Might as well tag 'long with me. All we need's a saddle horse apiece an' pack horses ta carry supplies. We can make Nevada in ten days, two weeks tops."

A week later, a local rancher came by and watched Herman and Ray take turns bucking out horses. One horse in particular caught his attention, a gentle brown gelding that refused to buck. Ray claimed ownership of the gelding and the rancher told him, "I like that horse. If you trade him to me I'll let you have a horse I brought in off the desert. The boys call him Cholla. Nobody's been able to stick on him. I don't believe he can be ridden."

That statement piqued Ray's interest and he quickly made the trade. The rancher delivered Cholla, a stocky, hard-muscled, bald-faced bay the following day. "I picked him up over in eastern Oregon, at the MC ranch, one of the biggest cattle outfits in the country. None of them buckaroos over there could stick. You got your work cut out for you, Ray. No doubt about it, this is one mean horse. He'll try to kill you."

Cholla had to be roped and thrown to the ground to saddle. As he regained his footing Ray swung aboard and for a moment the horse seemed dazed, as if he did not know what to do. Ray shifted his weight, flexed his knees and dug with his spurs. In response Cholla tried to turn himself inside out. He bucked high and hard and stayed with it for a long time. Ray was determined. He took everything Cholla had to offer and when the outcome was settled, and the outlaw had stopped bucking, Ray rode him around the pasture until it appeared the horse had reformed and become as gentle as a pet.

Bill Hooper, a local farmer and rancher who had heard the Vowell brothers were bucking out wild horses and was in attendance that day, fell in love with the bald-faced bay. "He would make a dandy horse for my brother," he said.

Ray told him in all honesty, "Don't believe your brother could ride him."

"If a kid like you can ride him, holy smokes, my brother can sure enough take care of business. I'll give you thirty-five bucks for him."

Ray sold Cholla and delivered him to Hooper's brother, with a warning. "This horse is flat out mean."

Less than a week later Bill led Cholla into the barn yard at Laird Landing. "You were right, Ray. This is a dirty, rotten excuse for a horse. My brother was riding him, leaned down to open a gate, got throwed and this horse tried to kick him in the head on the way past. And then the next morning, I was there, saw this with my own eyes, my brother tried to mount and even before he could get settled Cholla bucked him up onto the roof of a lean-to. My brother sat right there on the roof and told me to get rid of that horse. Said he didn't want him on the place.

"Keep the thirty-five bucks I gave you. Take him back."

"I don't really want him," said Ray.

"If I keep him I'll have to shoot him. I don't want to shoot him. Tell you what, I'll give you twenty-five more if you take him off my hands," said Bill.

The Vowell brothers sold their wild horses as they broke them. But Cholla they kept. One warm day in March Bill Hooper paid another visit to Laird Landing. "I've got a herd of cows and the first of the month I plan to trail them to Goose Lake. Take five days, six maybe. You fellows interested in buckarooing for me? Chance to see new country."

Ray had already signed on to work that spring for Corpening & Donavan but Herman and Fred Westfall jumped at the chance to drive a herd of cattle to Goose Lake. After Bill departed Fred said, "If I get that far I might as well keep goin'. Moffett Cattle Company, out of Paradise Valley, Nevada, said they wanted me ta come back ta work for 'em. All I gotta do is show up an' the job's mine. Come with me, Herman. They're always in need of a decent bronc buster."

"I'll think about it."

The only horse Herman had at his disposal was Cholla. Even though he was an outlaw he was big and strong and if Herman were constantly on his guard Cholla would make an adequate mount.

Herman rode Cholla to the blacksmith in Malin to be shod. Cholla would have none of it. The blacksmith resorted to an old and tested method of shoeing a bad horse. He brought out a wagon wheel, threw Cholla and tied each foot to a different spoke. When he finished Cholla was wearing four new shoes and no one had been injured in the ordeal.

Bill, Herman, Fred and a hired hand named Harry Miller started the drive with 210 head of pregnant cows. It had been a hard winter and as soon as the cattle got onto the south-facing foothills where the tender young grass was coming up, all they wanted to do was graze. The first day they made a meager seven miles before setting camp. The following day was only eight miles. The third day the cattle were more inclined to move and were trailed twenty miles to Steele Swamp ranch.

Hubert Morelock, the ranch foreman, was waiting for them at the lower end of the meadow and helped push the cattle through the gate and into the Wrango field near the ranch house. His wife Emma prepared a big supper of meat, potatoes and canned corn that tasted as fresh as if it had been picked that day. After the meal Fred and Harry adjourned to the bunkhouse. Bill stayed to visit. Herman went for a ride up the hill to watch the sun set. As it dropped behind the mountains the clouds came alive with colors; yellow, gold, red, orange and crimson. The vibrant hues hung in the sky like glorious fireworks. Slowly the colors began to fade. Herman looked over the thousand acres of meadow and knew in his heart he had found the most perfect spot in the entire world. If he could live here, in this breathtakingly beautiful setting, on this secluded and productive cattle ranch, he told himself he would be content and happy every day of his life.

The following morning, after eating Emma's hearty breakfast, they drove the cattle off the meadow grass. Hubert rode lead, pushing away any cattle that carried the Pitchfork brand. After several hours he turned back for Steele Swamp. Fred was riding drag and he called out, "How far is it ta Willow Creek Ranch?"

"Twelve miles," Hubert called back.

"It was seventeen when we started," grunted Fred. "Ya mean ta say we only come five miles?"

"That's what I mean to say." Hubert spun his horse and he rode away.

Fred laughed out loud, "That ol' goat is tryin' ta pull my leg. I say we only got five miles ta go. That's what I say." But they rode on and soon came to a sign that pointed northeast and read, "Willow Creek Ranch – 12". Fred concluded, "Flat can't believe it. He was right an' I was wrong. First time for ever'thin'."

The day became uncomfortably hot and the larva of the warble fly began to come alive on the backs of many of the cows. They hatched under the skin and ate their way to the surface. In pain and agony the cows curled their tails over their backs and ran in search of brush or low limbs to rub away their discomfort. Herman and Fred were constantly having to chase down cows and bring them back.

Herman ran Cholla after a cow that darted into a thicket of mahogany. They followed until the mahogany grew so thick Cholla could go no farther. Herman dismounted, tied his lead to a stout limb, and went after the cow on foot. He managed to turn her and get her headed back down the hill toward the herd. He returned to Cholla, coming in just behind him. Herman knew better, knew that he should work his way around to the front of his horse, but that would require crawling on his hands and knees through the mahogany wall. He figured Cholla was tired from three days of riding and elected to take a chance. He spoke to Cholla, letting him know he was coming up from behind. Herman came close enough to reach and pat Cholla's rump. A pair of hooves suddenly struck him in the stomach, propelling him backwards into the tangle of mahogany. He broke off limbs and landed on the hard ground. He lay there for a moment, trying to catch his breath and taking an inventory to make sure he was not bleeding and all the parts worked; arms, legs, shoulders, neck. When he was satisfied he was still in one piece he got to his hands and knees and crawled in a semi-circle, coming to Cholla from the front as he should have done in the beginning.

That afternoon they reached Willow Creek Ranch and again were treated hospitably with a fine supper and a comfortable bunk. They hoped to make Goose Lake the following day and had high hopes of accomplishing that when they reached a ridge top and spotted a large body of water in the distance. Bill claimed it had to be Goose Lake. But the landmarks were not where they were supposed to be. He told Harry to scout ahead and when he spotted the headquarters of Lakeside Ranch he was to double back. Harry headed toward the lake with the pack horse trailing behind.

Towering anvil-shaped thunderheads boiled up and took over the sky. The wind began to gust and kick up grit. The day grew dark and ominous. Lightning suddenly flashed from the dark-bellied clouds. The ground shook. Cattle bellowed. Horses danced. Rain splattered with such force the drops seemed to have more substance to them than mere water. The men pushed the herd onward and soon came to a small field enclosed by a wire fence. Over the noise of the storm Bill shouted to corral the cattle.

The final cow was squeezed through the gate and Herman turned his attention to roping sagebrush and limb wood and dragging it behind Cholla to where Fred was starting a fire. The three men stood in the rain watching flames flicker and wondering what was keeping Harry. "I'm having a few doubts," Bill finally admitted. "I don't remember hills like this anywhere near Goose Lake. Boys, we might have taken a wrong turn."

A few moments later he spoke again. "I don't like the thought of a man off by himself, especially when he has the packhorse with our food and bedrolls. Herman, why don't you go see if you can find Harry. Bring him back."

By then the light was beginning to fail and rain was coming down with a mean urgency. Herman untied Cholla from the juniper. He had the lead in his hands and was coiling it when Cholla suddenly reared and struck with his front feet, pawing the air and striking at Herman's chest. Herman was lucky. The only damage was a ripped shirt.

"That horse is going to be the death of you yet," shouted Bill. Herman ignored him and swung into the saddle. As he traveled he could make out shapes of rocks and juniper trees, but in the storm and the fading light they became less and less distinct. Every once in a while he called Harry's name but the way the rain pressed in, Herman doubted his voice could be heard a hundred yards away. At one point he brought his hand up and wiggled his fingers. It was too dark to see them and he turned Cholla around and gave him his head, trusting the horse to return to the cattle and the other horses.

They came out of the night to the light of the pathetic little campfire beneath the spreading juniper. Herman pulled his saddle and joined the other men, telling them he had been unable to locate Harry. After that there was very little to be said. They were going to spend a miserable night in the cold and wet. The only sounds were the fire, the cattle slopping around in the gumbo mud and rain continuing to drip with irritating regularity.

Herman fell asleep near the fire. He awoke once when Bill threw a few chunks of limb wood on the coals. It was still dark when birds began to sing and Herman came fully awake from his paralyzed, dreamless sleep. His eyes felt like bits of ash and grit had become imbedded under the lids. He was wet, cold, stiff and sore. But the morning dawned bright and clear and the air was full of just-washed freshness. Distant hilltops appeared with startling clarity. His stomach growled and a stab of pain told him he was hungry.

"Let's get a move on," said Bill. "I thought about it all night and I know where we went wrong. There by Round Mountain we veered south when we should have gone east."

Fred was having a devil of a time working the kinks out of his old back. He wanted to know, "How fer back?"

"I don't know," grunted Bill. "A ways."

Harry caught up with them a couple hours later. He claimed he had bedded down under a rock ledge when it got too dark for him to find his way back to the cattle and admitted he had built a fire, ate a filling dinner and spent a warm, dry night hunkered under the protective ledge.

Fred wanted to know, "Ya got any food on that packhorse?"

"Ate it all. Wasn't that much left anyway."

The only agreeable thing about the day was that the sun was warming the air and drying things out. Around noon a rider from the Lakeside Ranch met them. "When you didn't show up, the boss figured you was either lost or havin' trouble. He sent me to see if I could find you. Looks like I got the job done."

At 5 o'clock they drove the cattle onto the Goose Lake pasture. Since the Lakeside Ranch headquarters was several miles away and the men had not eaten for a day and a half, the cowboy advised, "You'd be better off ridin' to the Fletcher Place. It's not but a little ways yonder in that direction." He pointed to the northwest. "Couple of government trappers been stayin' there. You know how the government feeds its employees. If I were you, that's sure 'nough the direction I'd head."

Without cattle to drive the four men made good time to the Fletcher Place. The trappers were not there but Bill opened the cabin door and led the way inside. Shelves lined one wall, each shelf stocked with canned goods. Hopper said, "I wish the trappers were here. Since they're not I say dig in. Eat what you want. I'll make it right."

That night the cowboys ate until their hunger had been satisfied and slept on cots in the lean-to. Sleep came quickly. But in the middle of the night they awakened to the sounds of boots reverberating like rifle shots off the floorboards. A match was struck, a flame flickered and lit a kerosene lamp.

"Looks like we got company," said a voice.

"Sure does," said another.

Bill jumped up, stumbled from the lean-to into the dimly lit cabin as he tried to explain, "We were driving a herd of cattle to Goose Lake. We ran out of food. Me and my boys hadn't had anything to eat since day before yesterday. I told them to fix what they wanted. I'm afraid we ate you out of house and home but I'll make good. I'll replenish everything."

"Fine by us," said one of the trappers.

The second offered, "We're just sorry we didn't have a better selection for you."

In the morning the trappers fixed breakfast. The cowboys ate and headed for home. When they reached the top of the Goose Lake rim Fred Westfall pulled up. "This is where we part company. I'm headin' fer Nevada." He turned to Herman. "Ya made up yer mind? Comin' with me? I wouldn't mind the company."

At that moment Bill chose to share information he had been withholding. "Herman, when we spent the night at Steele Swamp, Hubert Morelock asked if I was keeping you on. I told him I'd like to but I didn't have work enough. He said he liked the way you handled yourself. Said he might be able to find you a job with old man Dalton. He owns the Pitchfork. Runs 4,000 head from the home ranch east of Malin. They range all through the Devil's Garden. If you do catch on it'd be a good job, steady, too. Don't get me wrong. I'm not trying to talk you out of going with Fred. You make up your own mind."

"Ain't got time fer jawbonin' about what might or might not be. I got miles ta go an' times a wastin'," drawled Fred as he leaned one forearm on his saddle horn. "Well, Herman, ya comin' ta Nevada with me or ain't ya?"

Herman stalled. He recalled the sun setting over Steele Swamp and his thought that he could feel comfortable and content in such a place. "I might want to look into that job with Mr. Dalton. If it doesn't work out I'll come down. How'd that be, Fred?"

"Suit yourself," said Fred. He picked up his reins and with a clicking sound, tongue against his teeth, he started his horse forward. The packhorse trailed obediently behind.

The last Herman saw of the old man was from several miles away. The rider and the two horses were skylined as black silhouettes on the top of the ridge. Fred dropped out of sight. The packhorse was poised there for a moment, the lead rope came taut, he threw his head and followed.

On the ride back from Goose Lake the three cowboys spent the night at Steele Swamp and Herman talked to Hubert about the buckarooing job. "Frank Pratt is the buckaroo boss," explained Hubert, "but Mr. Dalton does the hiring and firing. One time Frank convinced Mr. Dalton to hire a fellow he met, a half-breed from over on the coast. Not a bad buckaroo but a drinker and when he drank he loved to fight. Mr. Dalton is a great judge of character and had some reservations about hiring him. Frank kept pushing for it. George didn't last but a couple weeks. Got in a fight in the bunkhouse at the home ranch and that was the end of it. Down the road he went."

"Do you know if Mr. Dalton would hire me?" Herman asked.

"Not for a solid fact. After you were here I called him, said you were pretty young but that you could handle a nasty horse and get a full day's work out of him. He told me to send you down, he'd talk with you."

SEVEN

Herman rode Cholla to the home ranch on May 1, 1936. He passed the white two-story colonial that Mr. Dalton had built in 1922 and continued to the barn. When his horse had been tended he walked back to a building near the house where Hubert said Mr. Dalton had an office. Herman climbed the steps and was about to knock on the door when a voice boomed, "Come on in."

Mr. Dalton was not a particularly tall man but he was built solidly for being sixty-two years old. His ruddy complexion proved he spent a good share of his time outdoors. He extended his hand to Herman. His grip was firm and full of confidence.

Herman had practiced his delivery on the thirty-mile ride from Steele Swamp. "Mr. Dalton, my name is Herman Vowell. I was helping drive cattle to Goose Lake and spent time with Hubert Morelock. He said to come see you, that you might be in the market for a buckaroo."

"Have a seat," said Mr. Dalton. He dropped his bulk into a leather chair behind a massive desk partially hidden by stacks of papers. It was Mr. Dalton's own unique filing system and he knew exactly where everything could be found. "Hubert claimed you were nothing short of an expert on horseback. But tell me, what kind of ranch experience do you have, young man?"

"I've been around cattle, Mr. Dalton, but I don't profess to know everything. I'm a quick learner and once I've got it in my mind I don't forget."

"My buckaroos spend most of their time in the hills, riding and working cattle. They don't get to town but once every few months. That a problem?" asked Mr. Dalton.

"Not in the least," said Herman. "I prefer being out to being in."

"Buckaroo wages are $35 a month. I furnish board and room. Generally room is a bedroll under the stars."

"Perfect," grinned Herman.

"I'll give you a try. The man you answer to, besides me, is my buckaroo boss, Frank Pratt. Do what he says. Can you start first thing in the morning?"

"Yes sir. I need to get myself a bedroll that's a little more comfortable. That's about it. And I have to call Mother, let her know I won't be coming home for a while. Tomorrow is her birthday. One thing though – about the pay. Suppose if I'm not here to collect it you could hold half what I've got coming and send the rest to Mother? She lives in Klamath Falls. I'll write down the address."

"You want your mother to have half your wages?"

"Yes sir. Dad died and I've still got a brother and two sisters at home. Since I was big enough to get a job I've always tried to help out. My older brother, Ray, is the same way. We do what we can."

"An admirable quality," said Mr. Dalton. He could not stop himself from smiling a little. He knew he had made a wise choice in hiring this young man. He was not only well-mannered and respectful, but his family came first with him.

"Find an empty cot in the bunkhouse. You'll be working out of the home ranch here for a day or two. Pick yourself five or six good horses from the cavvy. Frank will tell you which ones aren't already claimed."

He stood then, and extended his hand to Herman. "Welcome aboard, Herman. If you ever have a problem, feel free to come to me. My door is always open."

"Thank you, Mr. Dalton, sir." As Herman went out the door and down the short flight of stairs, he could feel his chest swell with the pride of accomplishment. He was now employed by one of the best outfits around and for the first time in his young life he could see that he had a real future. His sole ambition in life had come true. He was a full-fledged buckaroo.

Frank Pratt, buckaroo boss of the Pitchfork Ranch, was described as being so short he was cut off at the pockets. Another description said Frank was so skinny, if he closed one eye he would be mistaken for a needle. Frank Pratt had spent nearly every minute of his fifty-six years in the saddle and as a result he was bow-legged to the point he could stand and straddle a whiskey keg. He smoked a pipe and had the unsightly and filthy habit of drooling when the pipe was in his mouth. Every so often he wiped at the dribble and the back of his hand was permanently stained tobacco-juice brown. He was missing his natural teeth, but had been fitted with dentures.

During one of Herman's first cattle drives an old cow balled up under a juniper tree and refused to move. Frank rode close to her and bellowed "Yaahh!" to try and force her to move. His false teeth shot from his mouth, into a high arc that brought them tantalizingly close, but just beyond reach. They landed on the jagged edge of a chunk of basalt and broke in two with a sharp cracking noise. Frank gummed it for the remainder of the summer. And his lack of teeth caused him to slobber tobacco juice even more.

One morning, the buckaroos were camped at Wildhorse with a few cowboys from the SX Ranch. Frank was cooking and sent the new man, Herman, to the reservoir with a pail to fetch water for coffee. When he returned Herman set the pail down and looked in Frank's direction. Frank was gumming his pipe, leaning over making biscuits. An appalling slobber dangled from his mouth. Frank tried to backhand it but not soon enough and the caustic stream fell directly into the biscuit dough. Frank did not notice, or did not care. He kept working the dough.

At breakfast Frank handed Herman the plate of biscuits. Herman passed them on.

"Herman, ain't you gonna have none of my biscuits?"

"Not this morning."

"Why not? You're always good for three or four. Come on, have a biscuit."

Herman shook his head, lied, "I don't feel so hot. I'm about half sick."

"These biscuits'll cure anything you've got."

"I'm not hungry, Frank, really."

"Come on."

"No."

In spite of Frank's occasional shortcomings he was a good man who felt a responsibility to pass on his considerable knowledge to the generations of buckaroos who would follow in his footsteps. As they worked he often related stories to Herman about how the various landmarks had been named and events that had occurred there.

One of Frank's favorite stories, handed down by an old cowboy he had known, was an account of the winter of 1879-80. Winter began with an early snowstorm followed by a powerful Chinook that swept up from the south and melted the top layer of snow. Hard on the heels of the warm wind came an Arctic front that settled in over the country and froze the snow into a crust as hard as steel. Cattle bunched up in the thickets, eating the willows to the level of the snow and the pine tree bark as high as they could reach. They humped their backs against the cold and their bellies distended from lack of feed. When they faltered and went down they could not rise.

Jesse Carr had burned the Pitchfork brand on several thousand calves that fall but when spring arrived only 53 head had survived. Frank puffed his pipe and thoughtfully proclaimed they were long overdue for another winter like that.

One time they rode past the little cabin at Mammoth Springs and Frank commented, "Zane Grey lived there in 1920. He wrote *Forlorn River* in that cabin. When he first came to the country he stayed at the bunkhouse on the home ranch. But one night he was cleaning his rifle and it went off. The slug traveled through the wall and put a hole in the water trough. After that Mr. Dalton told Zane Grey he was no longer welcome. So he lit out, rode around Clear Lake and settled here. Twenty years ago it was a pretty nice cabin. He wandered all over the country, picking out interesting sites, writing about them. Did you ever read it, his book, *Forlorn River*? Forlorn River is really Lost River."

Herman shook his head.

"Part of the book is about a rich fellow who owns this big spread. He is meaner than heck. There's no doubt he is describing the Pitchfork Ranch and Mr. Dalton. Could have been he did that because Mr. Dalton threw him out and he was wanting to get back at him. I don't know that for positive.

"I do know Mr. Dalton asked me if I had read the book. I said I had. He said not to believe everything I read. Said there was absolutely no truth to it. Said when the homesteaders started going broke, in about 1918, he paid cash for their property. Paid each and every one of them. Otherwise they would have left with nothing. Mr Dalton told me straight, 'The book says I cheated them out of their property. I never did such a thing.'

"While Zane Grey was living at Mammoth Springs he saw the cowboys capture California Red. He was a stud horse.

Beautiful. All the cowboys used to talk about him, dream they would be the one who got a rope on him. The way it came about happened in the winter of '20. Ice, a foot deep, covered Clear Lake. The cowboys sharp-shod their horses and ran California Red out onto the ice. California Red kept slipping, losing his footing, falling. The cowboys roped him, brought him in and tamed him.

"Zane Grey told all about that in his book. That was the high point of the story, describing that horse and how he was captured. In my opinion, after that the book ran out of steam and fizzled."

At Fiddler's Green, near Clear Lake, Frank showed Herman where the headquarters of the Pitchfork had once been. All that remained was a dilapidated house, a number of corrals and the blacksmith shop. Frank jerked a thumb toward the blacksmith shop and said that was the place where Captain Jack, chief of the Modoc tribe, was brought after his capture.

"Lot of bad blood between the Modocs and the white folks who came in to settle the country. The government tried to force them onto the reservation with the Klamath tribe but the Modocs and the Klamaths were enemies from back before time began. Captain Jack and his followers pulled out and moved down into this country. When the soldiers came after them they retreated to the Lava Beds. It was a natural fortress and fifty warriors managed to hold off the entire United States Seventh Cavalry. When General Canby called for peace council the Indians, under a white flag, murdered him. Only general ever killed in the Indian wars.

"After that Captain Jack tried to escape from the Lava Beds but the soldiers ran him down, caught him below Steele Swamp, about where Boles Creek runs into Willow Creek. They brought him to Fiddler's Green and, according to what the blacksmith told me, he said Captain Jack and a band of his men had visited headquarters a year or two before the war and demanded payment to the tribe. Jesse Carr refused. As Captain Jack left he told the blacksmith, 'One day you leave this place'. When the blacksmith put shackles on Captain Jack, he reminded him of the conversation and pointed out that one of them was sure enough leaving the place. The soldiers took Captain Jack to Fort Klamath, hung him and three of his braves.

"Supposedly what happened was someone cut off Captain Jack's head, took it around the country in an exhibit and charged people a dime for a look. Always did think that was a little more than was necessary. But in those days folks had pretty strong opinions about the war and all the killings that had taken place."

Herman valued Frank's colorful stories. Knowing the history firmly tied him to the land and instilled in him a respect for those who had come before him. One time Frank said, "Maybe in 50 years they'll be telling stories about you and me. Think they will?"

"Yeah, someone will probably write a book and call it *The Wisdom of Frank Pratt.* Folks won't know if any of it is true or if it's all a bunch of tall tales."

As the seasons progressed the Pitchfork buckaroos drifted across the Devil's Garden; pushing cattle onto better grass, doctoring any cows that needed it, moving on. They stayed for a few days or a few weeks at cabins and camps scattered across a range of nearly 2,000 square miles. Herman loved it all; the days in the saddle, the horses, the cattle, the men. He especially enjoyed the freedom of constantly being on the move, seeing new country, discovering what was over the next ridge.

Later that summer they returned to Wildhorse camp. The water was down in the reservoir and near where Herman had dipped the pail of water for Frank several months earlier, was a dead horse that had been there a long time, its hide pulled away from bleached bones.

When fall arrived the Pitchfork buckaroos trailed the three-year-old steers to the railroad stockyard in Malin where they were loaded into cattle cars and sent to markets in California. After the last steer was shipped the men spent several weeks working the cows and calves at the home ranch. It was Herman's responsibility to rise early each morning and bring in the cavvy so the buckaroos could pick out their saddle horse for that day. Cholla was part of the cavvy and, as usual, caused trouble; biting horses and kicking the corral rails.

One morning after Herman corralled the cavvy he saw Mr. Dalton waiting for him. They exchanged greetings and then Mr. Dalton came to the point. "That horse you rode in on, you call him Cholla, I've been watching him. From everything I've seen he is as full of venom as a rattlesnake in July.

"Herman, you ride that horse every five or six days, but we wrangle every single day. One of these mornings he is going to hurt one of the other horses or a buckaroo. I wonder if you'd get rid of him. We have plenty of dependable horses around here."

Herman did not want to sell Cholla. He appreciated the outlaw's spirit and the challenge of riding such a horse. But he could also see Mr. Dalton's point. There was a risk in keeping Cholla. If the boss did not want such an animal on the ranch, it was his right. Herman was not going to make Cholla an issue. Like Mr. Dalton said, there were plenty of horses. It did not make sense to get attached to any one of them. Herman replied, "Yes sir, Mr. Dalton."

Herman sold Cholla to a stock contractor who thought the gelding might become a great rodeo bucking horse like Midnight or Angel. The first time Cholla was put in a chute he fought as though he had never seen a human being, fought until the gate opened and the flank cinch came tight. And then Cholla stepped forward into the arena like a cat stepping in a puddle of water. He cautiously pawed the dirt to test it, then stood still and no amount of coaxing could induce him to buck.

The contractor sold Cholla to a young couple looking for a dependable buggy horse. They soon learned, after Cholla had torn up their buggy, the purchase had been a terrible mistake. They sent him to the chicken feed plant. Herman felt responsible and wished he had found Cholla a better home.

When snow began to fall Mr. Dalton sent Herman to help Hubert feed the thousand head of cows wintered at Steele Swamp. Herman assumed he would stay in the bunkhouse, but when he arrived he found an old man, who had long ago outlived his usefulness, holed up in there. He never bathed, smelled as bad as a sheepherder's socks, and could not string two words together without one of them being a cuss word. Hubert did not want an impressionable young man like Herman living with such a wretched old coot. He caught Herman as he was putting his horse away and told him, "I want you to bunk in the house. Emma has a bedroom fixed for you. It's upstairs and might be a trifle cold of the mornings but you'll survive."

That first evening, and every evening after, Emma warmed two sad irons on the stove, wrapped them in a pillowcase, and handed them to Herman to place under the covers at the foot of his bed. No matter how cold it got, and there were nights when it was down to 40 below, his feet were always warm.

Hubert and Herman, with very little help from the old man, spent their days harnessing workhorses, pitching loose hay from stacks onto a sled, feeding the cows. Every time a storm moved through one of them fed while the other rode the telephone line and repaired it where it had come down. Sometimes that required riding 40 or 50 miles in a long day. But it was a job that had to be done because Mr. Dalton insisted on being able to communicate with Steele Swamp at any time.

On Herman's 21st birthday, February 1, 1937, Mr. Dalton called the ranch. He told Hubert a friend had flown over the Devil's Garden the day before and spotted a number of cows kegged up around a spring six miles south of Steele Swamp. The spring was providing them water but there was no feed. They were slowly starving. "I want Herman to ride out and bring them in. Have him take a good horse. It might be tough going. The snow is drifted and deep in spots."

Herman rode a black horse named Light Foot. He was strong and stout and had a lot of go in him, but he could not be controlled without spurs. Herman's spurs fit only over his light-weight boots but Herman figured it was better to have his feet a little cold than to get thrown and have to walk home.

He left the barn with a north wind at his heels. By the time he reached the cattle and turned them toward the ranch it had begun to snow. Light Foot trudged through the deepening snow, head down into the wind, his muzzle becoming spindled with frost and his eyes rimmed with ice. Frozen saddle leather squeaked against the wooden tree. Herman felt each step of the horse clear through to his bones. His nostrils froze to the post of his nose and he was forced to breathe through his mouth. He fought to stay awake. He sang a little, hummed, pounded his gloved hands together. But he could do nothing for his feet. They hung in the stirrups like meat in a locker, getting colder and colder and colder.

The leading edge of the front moved through, the wind let up some but the snow fell harder and faster. It curtained off the world. Herman could hear his breath rattle in his lungs. His eyebrows puffed with frost. His feet were past the point of pain. There was no feeling in them at all and he was not even sure they were still attached to the ends of his legs. As night descended the snow stopped, the sky cleared and the air became heavy and still and bitterly cold.

The cattle pushed through the gate and into the corral at Steele Swamp. They immediately went to a pile of hay and began feeding. Herman dismounted, closed the gate and could not remount. He held onto the saddle horn and Light Foot dragged him to the barn. He managed to pull his saddle and started for the house, swinging his legs like wooden posts. Hubert met him on the way.

"What happened to you?"

"Froze my feet."

"Why didn't you get off and walk?"

"Snow was too deep."

"You need to take off your boots. Walk in the snow

barefooted. That will help thaw them. Otherwise, you come in by the stove, they heat up too fast and it's gonna hurt like the dickens."

Herman sat on the ground. Hubert pulled off Herman's boots and socks. He even gave him a hand up and Herman shuffled in the direction of the house. Emma stuck her head out the door, saw what was going on and shouted at Herman, "Get in here this minute. Walking around like that is going to freeze your feet even worse."

Hubert laughed. He thought his practical joke was funny. Emma did not. She scolded him, "Hubert, you should be ashamed of yourself." She took control, made Herman sit in a chair and soak his feet in a pan of coal oil. As they began to thaw they hurt so badly Herman dug grooves in the arms of the chair with his fingernails. When the pain decreased to a throbbing ache Emma sat on the floor and rubbed circulation back into his feet. Long after Herman fell asleep she continued to work and by morning, though his feet were swollen and discolored, Emma thought she had probably saved most of his toes.

In the following days Herman's skin changed colors and sloughed off his feet and toes. It was replaced by soft, pink new skin. Herman promised Emma that when he got to town he would buy her something especially nice to express his gratitude. But Emma told him, "No, don't do that. I know how jealous Hubert can be. Seeing you walking again is all the thanks I'll ever need."

In March Mr. Dalton called Hubert and said he needed Herman to work cattle. Frank Pratt and a man to replace Herman were riding to Steele Swamp. He wanted Frank and Herman to drive any cow that did not appear pregnant, and weighed between 700 and 900 pounds, back to the home ranch. He made it clear those were the only cows he wanted.

Hubert was a funny sort. He could be extremely moody. He either liked a person or he did not and he had never liked Frank Pratt. When Frank and the new man arrived, Hubert was in one of his nasty moods. He instructed the new man to go with Herman and help feed. He told Frank he would give him a hand separating the cows.

Hubert purposely did not tell Frank that Mr. Dalton had called that morning and specified which cows he wanted. Every time Frank brought a cow that did not fit within the narrow parameters set by Mr. Dalton, Hubert called out, "Not that one," and turned the cow away.

After this happened several times Frank rode to where Hubert held the separated cows. "Mr. Dalton gave me instructions on what he wanted. I know what I'm doing so quit turning back the ones I bring out."

"You don't know what Mr. Dalton wants."

"I'm buckaroo boss of this outfit. I know."

"Well, I spoke with Mr. Dalton this morning and he told me exactly what he wants sent out. I'm the ranch manager. You're on my ranch. I guarantee you, not a single cow is going to leave here without my okay. So put that in your pipe and smoke it, old man."

Later, as Herman and Frank drove the cattle toward the home ranch Frank told Herman what had transpired. "If I could have dug a stick out of the snow I would have beat Hubert to death with it." He let it go at that but for the two days of the drive he stewed and brooded.

After they ran the cows into the field at the home ranch Frank rode directly to Mr. Dalton's office. He tied his horse to the hitching rail out front, marched up the steps and strode into the office. "I quit."

Mr. Dalton was stunned. "Why, Frank?"

Frank simply shook his head and walked away. He went to the bunkhouse, gathered his few belongings and was off the ranch before the supper bell rang.

The next day Mr. Dalton found Herman and told him, "I suppose you heard, Frank quit me."

"Yep."

"He went to work for Campbell. He quits me and goes to work for a neighbor as a regular hired hand. I know they aren't paying what I do." Mr. Dalton let that sink in. "You know he's been with me a long time. For the life of me I can't think of a single reason why he would up and quit. Do you know what might have set him off?"

Herman said, "Frank never told me what he was thinking. But on the way in I knew something was eating at him. He was awful quiet. That's about all I can tell you."

Several days passed and then one morning Mr. Dalton was waiting for Herman at the hitching rail. From the way he was wringing his leather gloves Herman knew he was doing some serious thinking. He called out, "Herman, suppose you could come in for a moment?"

When Herman stepped inside the office Mr. Dalton asked, "I know it's a little early but would you care for a drink?"

"No sir, I don't drink."

"I believe I'll pour myself a short one." He took a bottle of whiskey and a glass from one of the desk drawers and poured the glass three fingers full. He put the bottle away and drained the drink in two long sips. He wiped his mouth and, seeming to remember his manners, he invited Herman to sit down.

"Since Frank quit me I've had seven men apply for his job. Some mighty fine and capable men, I might add. But not one of them knows my operation, knows the range and how to get the most out of it." Mr. Dalton paused and rubbed his chin. "Over the past year I've kept an eye on you. You're the best buckaroo I have. I was wondering what you would think if I were to make you my buckaroo boss."

Herman did not know what to say. He was stunned. He started to thank Mr. Dalton for having so much faith in his abilities, for even considering him for such an important position, but self-doubt swept over him and he muttered, "Well gosh, I've only been over the range one summer and some of those trails I don't even know if I could find them again. I don't think I know it well enough...."

"I've found that a man can be around something all his life and never learn it all. I learn something new every day," said Mr. Dalton.

"I don't know if I could...."

Mr. Dalton stood. He placed his hands on his desk, leaned toward Herman and looked him straight in the eyes. "I realize you are young, and have limited experience. But I'm a pretty fair judge of people and in you I see someone who has a God-given ability with horses, is smart, a quick learner and a natural leader. I'm convinced you are the best man for the job, far and away the best man, and I propose this – if I were to help you when you needed help, would you be willing to take the job?"

Herman was quick to answer, "If you were to help me, Mr. Dalton, I'd sure as heck be willing to give it a try."

The following morning Mr. Dalton was once again waiting for Herman at the hitching rail but this time he conducted his business outdoors. "We need to hire someone to replace what you were doing. Now if I hire a man he works for me, but if you do the hiring he works for you. Got anyone in mind?"

Herman knew immediately. "My brother Ray. He's working for Corpening & Donavan but I'm sure I could talk him into coming to work here."

"I don't have anything to do with it," said Mr. Dalton, tugging at the brim of his hat. "Aunt Nonie is the meanest woman alive. If she thought I had a hand in hiring away one of her men, there's no telling what she's capable of doing. I don't need that. Herman, you talk to your brother. Work it out. Whatever you do, don't get that woman riled."

Ray stayed with Corpening and Donavan until they turned the cattle out on the range and came to work at the Pitchfork on May 2, 1937, his mother's birthday, and exactly a year after Herman went to work for Mr. Dalton.

Herman and Ray rode together and Herman knew he would never be the boss over Ray. He might tell him what needed to be done, might even suggest something, but he was never going to direct Ray as though he were an employee. They were equals. They were brothers.

Their first job together, with a number of other buckaroos, was to push 1,700 head of mother cows onto the range and kick them loose to summer on the flats and in the timbered ridges of the Devil's Garden. In the fall, when the days became shorter and the temperature began to get cold, those fat cows and their calves would migrate toward their home and the handouts of hay. That year Herman and Ray drifted from one season to the next, living the dream they had shared growing up – cowboys riding the open range.

Fall 1938 Hubert and Emma left Steele Swamp and moved to a small farm near Malin. Jerry Stratton took over as manager of Steele Swamp. He had buckarooed all his life and was as steady and dependable as they came, although he warned Mr. Dalton that someday he planned to have a ranch of his own. His wife, Ollie, became cook. She was short and plump, accustomed to rising before daylight and working hard until well after the sun went down. She cooked, cleaned, gardened, canned, cut kindling, hauled wood, kept the fire going, fed the chickens, gathered eggs, milked the cow and churned butter. Jerry and Ollie were a perfectly matched team to operate the ranch.

The old two-story ranch house at Steele Swamp had been used as a stop in the late 1800s for travelers on the Applegate Trail, an offshoot of the Oregon Trail. It was in dire need of repairs; the roof was missing shingles, the walls lacked insulation and there was no way to heat the upper story. The Strattons remodeled; removing the top floor and using some of the lumber to enclose the screened veranda and make a dining hall. They added cupboards and drawers and a counter in the kitchen. When the project was completed, the single-story ranch house proved to be a very livable home. It was easy to heat in the winter and cool in the summer.

That same year, Mr. Dalton conducted an experiment by

sending 400 yearlings and 250 two-year-old steers to winter pasture at the McDermott Ranch near Morgan Hill, California. He believed the cost of transporting cattle to warm-weather pasture would prove cheaper than holding them over and feeding hay. The summer of 1939 Mr. Dalton sent Herman to California to round up the three-year-old steers and transport them to market. That was when Herman met Betty.

EIGHT

Betty knew she loved Herman. That was an absolute. But when the winter of 1942 set in with a vengeance and isolated Steele Swamp from the outside world, she discovered a richer, more abundant and satisfying love than she ever thought possible. In her mind she likened it to a red rose that began to bloom, and hour by hour, day by day, the petals of love unfurled, becoming ever more glorious in their opulence and beauty.

Their first winter together Betty found she cherished doing little things for Herman; surprising him with cookies, greeting him when he came in from the cold with a cup of hot chocolate, giving him a kiss for no reason at all. Each morning she rose early to warm the kitchen and cook breakfast. Later, as she washed the dishes and went about the household chores she continually glanced toward the meadow where she knew Herman was working. Each time she caught a glimpse of him her heart fluttered. In the evenings they played games and talked.

Betty gave considerable thought to why her love for Herman continued to grow and concluded it was not merely the time they spent together, nor was it the agony of the hours they spent apart, but it was in their conversations. As she learned more about him, and the experiences that had helped to mold him into the man he was, she found him all the more fascinating and attractive.

The change from winter to spring seemed to take place overnight. One morning Betty stepped outside and was amazed at the transformation that had come so suddenly to Steele Swamp. Her senses were overwhelmed by the sights and smells. Black birds sang in the willows. Sandhill cranes trumpeted, pirouetted and leaped high in the air in their strange mating ritual. Ducks and geese chattered loudly. Mule deer and antelope grazed. A ground squirrel dug a hole. Hawks and eagles circled lazily in the sky. Grass grew. Camas flowered. The pungent sage gave off a musky fragrance.

All of this was such a contrast to the cold and sterile isolation of winter. This profusion of tangible life dazed Betty. She threw back her head, opened her arms and enjoyed this moment to the fullest. When Herman came in for lunch she told him how wonderful it felt that spring had finally arrived. She was so animated and ingenuous that he teased her. "Your first winter and you get a case of cabin fever. Tell you what, Sugar, soon as the road firms up, I'll take you to town. We can have dinner and catch a movie. Would you like that?"

"I guess." She did not sound convincing. "The past few months have been wonderful. I've never felt isolated because I was with you. I know you better now than I ever would have if we lived in town. I love it out here. And I love you."

Betty sat on Herman's lap, threw her arms around his neck and kissed him. She was still sitting there when a sharp rap startled them both. Ray flung open the door and stepped inside. "If I'm not interrupting you lovebirds I thought you might enjoy getting your mail." Ray tossed a canvas sack on the table.

Betty rushed to Ray, gave him an excited hug and turned her

attention to the mail bag. She opened it and dumped the contents onto the kitchen table, sorted the envelopes into three piles; bills, letters from friends and letters from family. Betty opened one letter immediately, read a few lines and announced, "Mom wants to come for a visit. How long before the roads are passable?"

"If the weather holds, a week, ten days," drawled Ray.

"And if we get a warm wind, a couple days," added Herman.

Leona spent two weeks at Steele Swamp. She helped Betty plant the garden and promised to come back for a visit during harvest to help with the canning. "It's a bigger job than you think. You have to wash and sterilize the Mason jars, prepare the vegetables, boil the water. It's messy and your kitchen is unbearably hot. You work to exhaustion. Though, if you have someone to share the work, it's not that bad."

Haying was only six weeks away and Betty told her mother she was nervous about having to cook for more than a dozen hungry men. Leona taught Betty the intricacies of preparing and cooking large, healthy meals. Before she went home she told her daughter, "I've worried about you being way out here in the middle of nowhere like this. But now I see that everything you wrote is absolutely true. You do love it here. This life suits you, Betty. But most of all you love Herman, and he loves you. I'm so happy for the both of you."

Ray interrupted his buckarooing to come to Steele Swamp and help round up the work horses for haying season. Harvesting a thousand acres of meadow hay required horse power. The ranch used big, stout Belgians that spent most of the year ranging on the Devil's Garden. Ray knew where the horses were kegged up and one morning he, Herman and Betty made a big circle and drove the herd to Steele Swamp. Over the next several days the foals were branded and weaned, the colts castrated and turned out on the range with the yearlings. The aged horses were separated into three groups: those that had been worked in the past and were fairly gentle were hitched to a wagon, driven and turned into one field; the green-broke horses were hitched to a breaking cart and driven until they could be trusted; and the young horses that had never been worked were put into the round corral, lassoed, laid on the ground, hobbled and tied to a post to halter-break them. One at a time Herman and Ray broke them to lead and to accept the harness. As they gentled they were hitched to the breaking cart and driven in tandem with a trusted horse where they learned to pull and respond to the basic commands of whoa, gee, haw and back.

Betty was not involved in the breaking process. Herman said it would be too dangerous so she stayed outside the corral and watched the brothers work, marveling at how they were able to take a wild horse and in a matter of hours, teach it to drive and accept the commands of a teamster.

One afternoon Betty brought Herman and Ray a pitcher of lemonade. "The two of you are worth your weight in gold."

Herman took a sip. "What happened, bottom fall out of the gold market?"

"I'm not kidding. You make it look easy. Why do the horses respond to the two of you the way they do?"

"Just got a knack," drawled Ray.

"It's more than that. I think you have a special way of communicating with horses that other men don't. You make a horse believe you will never hurt him, that you're only going to teach him; and, once he accepts that, accepts you, he will do anything to please you. I hope you realize God gave you both a very special blessing."

Herman handed Betty the empty glass. "Thanks, Hon. We're thankful." He paused. "Say, I'll be going to town day after tomorrow to round up a hay crew. Better start a grocery list. I'll pick up whatever you need.

"Mr. Dalton said most of the crew comes back year after year and the teamsters always want the same horses, the same set of harness and even the same machines. But I don't know, with the war going on it might be hard to find good help. My orders are to hire any local man willing to work and if I can't put a crew together I'm supposed to drive to Klamath Falls. Mr. Dalton said back during the first world war he had to hire men off bar stools. Sometimes, to entice them, he bought a bottle for the ride out here. I guess in the morning, when they sobered up, they would stumble out of the bunkhouse wanting to know where on God's green earth they were and how they happened to get here."

During haying Herman and Betty rose before daylight. Betty built a fire and started breakfast while Herman wrangled the fifty or sixty head of workhorses that would be used that day, half in the morning and the remainder in the afternoon. As soon as the teamsters ate breakfast they hiked to the corral with halters in hand. Herman roped their horses for them. When all the men and horses were out in the field Herman caught a bite of breakfast, saddled his horse and spent the remainder of the day overseeing the operation and trying to second guess where any problem might occur. If there was a runaway he rode at top speed and roped one of the horses, making sure he kept away from the machinery as he brought the team under control. While the men ate lunch Herman replaced the dull sickle blades on the mowing machines with sharp blades and, if there was time, he grabbed a quick bite to eat before returning to the field.

In the evenings after supper, Herman sharpened sickle blades on a foot-powered sandstone wheel. A can of water was rigged over the wheel to furnish a steady drip that lubricated the grindstone. It was an art to put the proper hone on a blade. Sometimes one of the hired men would lend a hand but their participation was never a guarantee. Always, when Herman was finally able to call it a day, he tumbled into bed completely exhausted.

Betty normally had an extra hour or so in the afternoons before she started dinner. She usually spent the time sitting on a blanket in the shade of a tree, watching the haying operation.

The mowing machines cut the hay and laid it flat on the ground where it cured in the sun and wind. After a few days it was ready to be raked into windrows and gathered by dump rakes into bunches. Buck rakes slid the bunched hay to the stack.

Betty often thought that if she could choose a job on the hay crew she would probably want to operate a buck rake. It looked like the most fun. The driver sat between and a little behind the team and steered. Long wooden teeth swept close to the ground, floating along, picking up hay and transporting it to the stack. Common sense and efficiency dictated each stack be kept to about 50 ton each. That way, if the hay happened to be a little green and ignited from spontaneous combustion, only one stack would be lost.

Betty watched the buck rake dump hay at the bottom of a slide, a wooden ramp positioned at the foot of the stack. A net made of light chains was in position in front of the slide and hay was moved onto the net. When the net was full a signal was given and the cable that ran from the net and over the stack was brought tight by a team fastened to a flat sled. Mounted on the sled was a trip mechanism and when the hay had been dragged up the incline to the top, the stackers shouted and the pull-down man kicked the trip and dumped the load. The stackers hollered to the pull-back man on the other side of the stack that they were clear of the net and he moved his horse forward, pulling the net to the bottom of the slide with a rope tied to his saddle horn. While he repositioned the net for the next load, the stackers pitched hay, building the stack, keeping the sides straight, rounding the top so the hay would lay flat and shed the rain and snow. Stacking took skill.

Betty faced the meadow, watching the action, listening to the horses nicker and the men shout, "Take her up," and "Pull her back." If the wind was right she could hear the rattle of the net on the slide, the clank of the dump rakes and sometimes the clickity-clack of the mowing machines as the blades glided back and forth. The sounds were like music and everything Herman had described to her about the operation was no longer ambiguous and confusing. Every piece of equipment, every horse, every man was necessary and watching them work was like seeing the whirling gears of a machine in motion.

One Sunday Betty and Herman enjoyed a picnic lunch on top of a stack. Up there a breath of wind always swirled around, the aroma of the hay was intoxicating, and the view of the meadow and beyond was simply fantastic. That afternoon Betty changed her mind. She did not want to operate a buck rake. She wanted to work on top of the stack.

Only a few days remained of haying season when buckaroos from the Pitchfork Ranch and the SX Ranch, including Ray, arrived at Steele Swamp. They had spent the summer making a big circle, working the cattle from both ranches that were intermingled on the Devil's Garden. They had moved from Willow Creek to Weed Valley, from Dobie Swale to Wildhorse and a half dozen camps in between. Steele Swamp was the end of that circle.

Their arrival doubled Betty's work. She cooked three meals a day for up to twenty-five men. When she had the opportunity she observed these newcomers and saw how different they were from the hay crew. They held themselves above the common working man. They were buckaroos and proud of it. They refused to sleep in the bunkhouse, choosing to throw their bedrolls on the ground, under the stars. They ate their meals together as far away from the hay crew as possible. At the table the hay crew talked noisily but the buckaroos were a quiet bunch, and when they communicated they spoke softly and only to each other.

Herman was considered a lifetime member of this elite group and, since several of the men had buckarooed with Betty when she first came to Wildhorse camp as Herman's bride, they accepted her, too. They kidded Betty, telling her that if she worked at it, she might make a decent camp cook, saying her pancakes weren't half bad, asking if she got scrambled eggs by squeezing the chickens. Their joking was always in fun.

One Saturday evening Les Morgan and Smoky Smith, a couple SX buckaroos, told Betty she could sleep in because they were going to fix Sunday breakfast. Betty came awake about 4 a.m. to the noise of slamming cupboard doors, banging pots and pans and kettles, clattering dishes and rattling utensils.

Herman always rose early to milk the cow and as he pulled on his pants Betty kicked back the covers. "I can't stand it any longer. From the sound of it they have used every pot and pan and dish we own."

"Best not bother them," advised Herman. "They have it in their mind to do something special for you. Enjoy the opportunity to sleep in for a change."

"I can't," wailed Betty. "They're destroying my kitchen."

"Try," said Herman. He pulled the covers over her and planted a kiss on her lips. "Try real hard."

Les and Smoky cooked ham, bacon and sausage, scrambled eggs, sourdough biscuits, thick sausage gravy, hash browned potatoes and pancakes. And when breakfast was over they accepted all the compliments, saddled their horses and rode away.

At dinner Betty confronted the cowboy cooks. "I do appreciate your allowing me to sleep in, but boys, you left such a mess it took me four hours before I could find my counter. From now on you may pass through my kitchen on your way to the table but I'll handle the cooking."

Les and Smoky laughed. Their fixing breakfast had been nothing more than a practical joke. They planned to make enough noise and dirty enough dishes that Betty would feel compelled to get up and take over. But she had not and the joke was on them.

When the cattle around Steele Swamp had been worked, the SX buckaroos returned to Alturas and the Pitchfork buckaroos went to the home ranch in Malin. Ray stayed on at Steele Swamp and nearly every morning he kidded Betty, complaining his eggs smelled like a wet hen had laid them, or that his pancakes were not quite done in the middle, or that they were so tough he had to use an axe to break off a chunk to eat.

One morning Betty took a round hot-pad, dipped it in pancake batter, cooked it on the griddle and served it to Ray. He tried to cut it with a fork. "Betty, your pancakes are particularly tough this morning."

"Are not," said Betty, "They're as light and fluffy as a cloud. Aren't they, Herman?"

Herman grunted. "Like a cloud."

Ray used his knife and could still not cut the pancake. He sawed back and forth and did not catch on until the willowy ends of threads showed. While Betty and Herman laughed, Ray felt the heat of his blood rising in his face and even the tips of his ears. Very deliberately he pushed his plate away, rose and strolled out of the house.

All that summer and fall Herman and Betty worked to make Steele Swamp as self-sufficient as possible. Betty raised a big garden, cooked the fresh produce to feed the men and canned the extra to carry them through the long winter. Herman butchered hogs, cured the hams, shoulders and bacon slabs in barrels of brine and smoked them. When they ran low on meat a steer was butchered and hung in the cool house. Herman milked the cow and Betty made butter and cheese. She fed the chickens and gathered eggs, but Herman killed the fryers. Betty could not bring herself to swing the hatchet and cut off their heads. What bothered her the most was the way they flopped around in a headless death dance. She could not even bear to watch but it did not disturb her, after Herman brought in the lifeless birds, to pluck them, singe the pin feathers and clean and cut them up for dinner.

NINE

The fall of 1943, the Navy took control of the Devil's Garden and ordered the evacuation of all civilians. Most of the land was owned by the federal government who granted the ranchers annual permits to graze their cattle on the range. Navy officials explained this vast expanse of juniper and sage was needed for the war effort, as a bombing and gunnery range.

Mr. Dalton used his influence to divide the Devil's Garden into two ranges and exclude Steele Swamp from the evacuation order. The southern range was centered at Clear Lake, where a practice target was anchored to simulate a Japanese battleship. Bombers dove on the target and released dummy bombs. The northern range began 400 yards east of Steele Swamp and extended forty miles to Goose Lake. It was a gunnery range for fighter pilots to practice shooting targets towed on long cables behind planes.

From Steele Swamp Herman and Betty, and Ray when he

was there, had a clear view as Navy bombers broke formation and dove on Clear Lake. Several times a day a plane passed overhead, flying east and towing a target, a squadron of fighter planes in pursuit. Sometimes the pilots could not resist getting a jump on the target, and began firing while they were over Steele Swamp meadow; or they opened up with quick bursts from their .50-caliber machine guns directly over the house.

The targets were simple wooden frames covered by heavy paper. Every once in a while a bullet cut the cable connecting the target to the plane and the target fluttered to the ground like a loose kite. Herman and Ray found several and brought them to the house as war souvenirs.

With Steele Swamp located so close to the gunnery range, it was only a matter of time before problems arose. One day two hired men were fixing fence on the meadow when a squadron of fighter planes flew over firing at a target. The bullets hit so close to the wagon that the team spooked and ran away. The men hiked to the house and told Herman, "Take us to town. We ain't goin' back out there. This is too much like being on the front line."

That year haying season was difficult and stressful. Most able-bodied men were overseas and those who remained seemed to be old, infirm or alcoholic. Herman spent more time running back and forth to town, trying to find men to work, than he did supervising the operation. Each day work was delayed until after the morning flights of fighter planes had passed and they were forced to quit early before the evening flights began. Haying took a couple weeks longer than normal.

On the return leg to their base in Klamath Falls the Navy pilots sometimes had unfired ammunition and they made strafing runs on the new haystacks. That was of special concern because every eighth round contained a tracer, an incendiary round, that could start a fire. Herman called the airbase and spoke to the officer in charge. "Sir, these pilots are plumb dangerous. They're going to start a fire or kill somebody."

"Mr. Vowell, we are involved in training Navy pilots to fly combat in the war. There's nothing I can do unless you call to say we've killed a civilian and you have a body to prove it."

Not long after that conversation, in the fall of 1944, a squadron of Hellcat Fighters passed over the ranch house. One of the planes was trailing black smoke. Betty called to Herman, "Look, that one is wounded."

The damaged plane peeled away from the formation, banked hard to the left and came down on the meadow, skidding wildly, sending up a tall rooster-tail of spray. It hit a hump of high, dry ground and tipped on its nose, teetering, precariously close to going over, and then settled back on its wheels.

Herman and Betty ran to the pickup. It took time to reach the downed plane because they had to skirt the wet spots. They met the pilot walking in their direction. He introduced himself as Ensign Walter Kee. He had not received a scratch from the crash landing but had snagged his jumpsuit and ripped a gaping hole in the material as he climbed through a barbed wire fence.

Ensign Kee called the base from the telephone at the ranch and informed his commanding officer where he landed, that the plane had blown its engine and sustained damage to its landing gear and propeller. Over supper Herman asked Ensign Kee, "When you are diving on the target what do you see? Do you see anything on the ground?"

"You're locked in on the target. That's all you see," said Ensign Kee.

"Tell you what," said Herman. "We would really appreciate if you would spread the word around the base. Tell the pilots there are people and cattle on the ground at Steele Swamp. And we really don't like being shot at."

"Yes, sir," said Ensign Kee.

Late that night three men arrived in a jeep to transfer the pilot back to the Navy base. One of the men, who said he was from New York City, commented he had never seen a road like the one they traveled over. "I thought trails like that went out of date with Daniel Boone."

Two men were left behind to guard the plane. Twenty-four hours later they were replaced and every twenty-four hours two more replacements were sent to Steele Swamp. Each new set of guards, as well as those departing, stopped at the ranch house. They wore overshoes, never thought to take them off at the door, and left muddy tracks from the door to the wood stove and to the table. They always asked for coffee, even though coffee was rationed and hard to get. They would bring sandwiches from the base meant for the guards they were replacing, but generally would have eaten them on the long drive to the ranch. Betty fixed a meal, or at least a sandwich, for every guard, whether he was coming or going, and she mopped up after them, too.

The Navy sent a ten-wheel truck with a mounted crane to retrieve the plane. It took a week for the truck to inch its way over the muddy roads to Steele Swamp and another four days to travel three miles to the site of the wreckage. Deep ruts were torn in the meadow and when they came to a gate too narrow for the truck to pass through, the fence was knocked down. It was not replaced.

They reached the plane, lifted it with the crane and set it on the bed of the truck. The extra weight added to their problems. Near Elder Spring the truck attempted to cross a levee and slid into a ditch. It took several days of hard work to get it back to level ground. The truck moved so slowly it might have remained in the meadow indefinitely but one night a warm wind blew in from the south and dried things enough that the driver was able to move the big rig to the road. As they neared the house Herman tried to take a photograph but one of the uniformed men stopped him.

"This is top secret. No pictures allowed," stated the soldier.

Herman retreated to the shop and as the truck lumbered past he pointed the camera in its direction and snapped several photographs through the window.

Barney Weaver joined the Navy fresh out of high school. He signed on because he felt a commitment to his country, but he also wanted to get out of Oklahoma and see the world. He signed on to fly airplanes and told the recruiter he was not interested in flying bombers and having the lives of others resting on his shoulders; he wanted to fly fighter planes and be alone in the sky. The Navy trained Barney as a fighter pilot but assigned him to fly bombers. They stationed him at the Klamath Falls Naval Air Station.

November 24, 1944 Barney piloted a TBF Avenger, a single-engine bomber, on a routine training mission to drop practice bombs on the target at Clear Lake. Benjamin Kauffman of Indianapolis, Indiana was the radioman and Edward Grohs of Lynbrook, New York was crouched in the gunner's compartment.

Barney was flying in second position in the formation. A few minutes before 10 o'clock that morning, the five planes began their bombing run on the wooden raft anchored on Clear Lake. They reached a dive speed of more than 220 knots, over the red line, and the vibration in the older plane Barney piloted caused him to make a quick decision. He slowed, breaking formation, and completed his run. The lead plane swept to the left and Barney followed. He moved to resume his position but the number three plane, piloted by Ensign H. P. McGee, had moved over and assumed that slot. Barney blindly pulled up into the formation.

A thud and a shudder ran through the spine of Barney's plane. Metal screeched as the propeller of McGee's TBF Avenger chopped off the tail rudder of Barney's plane, and the head and left arm of gunner Edward Grohs.

Barney fought the controls but there was nothing he could do. They were going down. He barked at his men to get the hell out and turned his attention to saving himself. The hatch lever was jammed. He threw his weight into it and the lever broke free, the hatch opened and Barney bailed out. He tumbled, dream-like, rolling down the wing of his plane, bumping his face. He felt no pain. And then he was clear of his plane and free-falling through the debris field. His chute snapped open. Barney hung under its protective canopy, oscillating from side to side, dispassionately watching the tangled bombers fall from the sky. One of them, Barney wondered if it were his, caught fire and trailed smoke. He looked around, another chute was open and almost to the ground. That meant two of them had survived. Four were dead. As the ground raced up to meet him he said the words aloud, "Four dead."

Herman and Ray were on the meadow feeding cattle. A few minutes after eleven o'clock a Navy Piper Cub flew over them, circled and dropped something that fluttered to the ground like a feather.

"What do you suppose that is?" said Herman.

"Looked like a piece of paper," said Ray. "Might be a note."

Herman stuck his pitchfork in the hay. "If it's a note it probably says they plan to use us for target practice." He laughed but there was a bitter edge to his humor. Only a few days before, as he came out of the barn, a low-flying fighter set off a burst of machine gun fire. The live rounds hit a stack of juniper posts a scant 30 feet from Herman and the line of fire led directly toward the house, but thankfully, ended before reaching there.

They found the note and Herman read it aloud to Ray. "Plane wreck seven air miles southwest of your location. Signs of survivors. Gather any medical supplies at your disposal. I will guide you to the wreckage."

"Having trouble keeping them in the air," said Ray blandly. "Want me to go? You can finish feeding."

Herman shook his head. "Hard to tell what's involved. A man alone might find himself in over his head. We'll go together. The cows have enough to tide them over. We'll throw in extra when we get back."

The Vowell brothers took the sled to the barn and unhitched the work team while the spotter plane circled impatiently. Ray saddled two horses; Herman hiked to the house to retrieve the first aid kit and tell Betty what was happening.

"Can I come along?" asked Betty.

"Absolutely not," said Herman. "No place for a woman."

"Honey, please don't take any unnecessary chances."

He kissed her. "I'm only concerned about planes in the air, not the ones on the ground. We'll be back when we can get back. Don't worry."

"You know I will."

A foot of snow had fallen on Election Day. It had started to melt in a recent warm spell and Herman and Ray found the going slow; the remaining snow was wet and soft and the adobe mud under it was slick and boggy. It took three hours to reach the China Wall south of Bump Heads. At that point a flare exploded, arcing several hundred feet and falling back to the ground. Herman and Ray rode in that direction.

When they returned to Steele Swamp, arriving well after dark, Herman tried to explain to Betty what they had seen, what it had been like. It was difficult for him to put into words. "We smelled it long before we ever saw it. Airplane fuel stinks to high heaven. Putrid. The planes were lying close together. One of them was smoldering with thick, black smoke coming from it. We were a quarter mile away. I was in the lead. My horse shied. I looked at what upset him and that's when I saw him – one of the men. He was missing his head and one of his arms. I got sick to my stomach, had to get off my horse. But it didn't seem to bother Ray all that much, he rode on in."

"What did you do, Ray?" Betty wanted to know.

Ray, never one to speak about serious matters without careful deliberation, took his time. "The two survivors, pilots as it turned out, were standing a ways apart. I think they blamed each other.

I imagine they were in shock. They were just kids, couldn't have been twenty, if they were that."

"What did they say?"

"One of them couldn't remember much of anything. The other one was a little more talkative. Said he was from Oklahoma. He had cuts on his face but the bleeding had pretty much stopped. He didn't know how the accident could have happened. Said he was pulling up and collided with the other plane. Said there had to be other survivors."

"Were there?"

"Naw," said Ray. "I checked. Found three bodies. Two were trapped in the plane that burned. Flesh smells mighty rank burned like that. My horse wouldn't go anywhere near there."

"What could you do for the pilots?"

"Not much of anything. A few band-aids for the one who had skinned his nose and chin. Gathered up some sagebrush. Got a fire going. Strange thing was those two pilots stood there at that fire and they never said a word to each other. Not a single word. We waited until the ambulance crew got there. They had Billy Dalton with them. He showed them the way in."

"Little Billy?"

"Yep."

The four-wheel-drive unit and rescue party, including a medical officer, were dispatched to the crash site from the air base sixty miles away. They reached a spot near Clear Lake by early afternoon but with no roads to follow, they soon became lost and mired in the mud. They radioed a request for the owner of the ranch to send a man who knew the country.

Mr. Dalton sent his fourteen-year-old son, Billy, to ride in with the rescue unit. They told him the location of the crash was near a rock wall, southeast of Bump Heads. Billy knew how to get there and directed them around the south side of Clear Lake and over a sloppy and rough trail. They arrived at the crash site shortly after sundown. Herman and Ray were told to return home.

The pilots rode in the front of the rescue unit and Billy and the bodies were placed in back for the trip out. It was close to midnight when they reached the Dry Lake road. Mr. Dalton was waiting for them. When Billy pulled himself free from the tangle of burned and mutilated bodies and stood in the glare of the headlights, Mr. Dalton thought he had never seen anybody as pale as his son. The Navy unit continued on and as soon as they were gone Billy held onto the bumper of his father's pickup and vomited.

"I wish you hadn't seen that," Mr. Dalton told Billy. "I'm sorry I sent you in there. I didn't know it would be that bad."

Returning to the crash site a few days later Ray looked inside one of the planes and found a shoe. He picked it up. The laces were neatly tied. The foot was still inside. Later, a sheepherder found a skull past the China Wall, at least a quarter-mile from the crash site. The Navy claimed the remains.

Herman and Ray removed the rear wheel off Barney Weaver's plane and made it into a wheelbarrow. They also took one of the .50-caliber machine guns. They fired it a few times with live rounds they found lying around on the ground at Steele Swamp. Betty said it was a federal crime for a civilian to have a machine gun in his possession, especially one salvaged from a military aircraft. Herman hid it in the hay loft.

Mr. Dalton usually tried to have the winter order of groceries at the Steele Swamp ranch by the end of deer season: but 1944 was an unusual year, with the early snow, the warm spell, the mud, the two plane crashes and more snow. The phone line was down for a number of days and when it was finally patched together Mr. Dalton called Herman. "I can make it as far as the

Kowolowski's place with my pickup. You bring the sled around and meet me there at noon tomorrow. Read me a list of what you need and I'll bring it."

The following day Ray fed the cattle while Herman hitched a work team to a sled. Betty had decided to make this an outing and packed a picnic lunch and gathered several blankets. The day was cool but the sun was out and the sky was gloriously blue. They circled the swamp to Sagebrush Butte and picked up the trail that would lead past Clear Lake. A formation of planes appeared overhead and Betty said, "They're making a run on the target. If we hurry we can watch them."

Herman coaxed the team into a trot. At the top of a rise he stopped them. The vantage gave a clear view of the target raft, anchored in the protected arm of Clear Lake at Fiddler's Green.

Six planes hung in a tight formation at 10,000 feet. Suddenly, the lead plane peeled off and started down. There was no wind. The only noise breaking the stillness was the high-pitched scream of the torpedo bomber. Betty held fast to Herman's arm. "My, he's going fast."

They expected the plane to drop its practice bombs, pull out of the dive, level off and return to the formation. But it continued straight down, engine roaring, wing tips whistling eerily. The plane split the skin of the water a few feet from the target. It hardly made a ripple, just a quick blurp of air that bubbled up and burst on the surface. A thin column of steam appeared and was gone. The lake lay still as a sheet of glass. There was no wreckage, no debris, not even an oil slick to provide evidence that a crash had occurred. Betty and Herman looked at each other and the horror in their eyes confirmed what they had witnessed.

Overhead the second plane made its run on the target, dropped its arsenal of practice bombs a few feet from where the first plane now rested, out of sight, wedged deep in the mud. Each plane in succession completed its run and returned to the formation high overhead. When the pilots discovered the lead plane missing they began to search. They buzzed in circles like a swarm of bees. When their fuel ran low they hurried west toward the naval base.

That evening the leader of Torpedo Squadron 41, Lt. J.P. Keigher, from Los Angeles, and crewman David Herget, from Talisheet, Louisiana, were officially listed as missing. The third crewman was safe. He had been picked up for stealing gas the night before and was in jail.

Mr. Dalton was waiting at the Kowolowski Ranch. Herman and Betty told him about the plane plunging into the lake and the others in the squadron searching in vain for some trace of it. Mr. Dalton said, "I'll call and let them know. They'll probably want to speak with you and try to pinpoint the wreckage."

They transferred the supplies to the sled and Herman and Betty started back for the ranch. Ray met them with the message that a Navy lieutenant had been calling and wanted them to return his call as soon as they came in. When Herman reached the lieutenant he said, "Oh my gosh, am I glad you had Mr. Dalton call. That plane just vanished. We looked and looked but never found a thing. We are putting together a team of divers. Could you show us where you think it went in?"

"Sure," said Herman. "It's just a few feet from where the target raft is anchored."

"That poses a problem," said the lieutenant. "The raft broke loose and is floating free."

"I can come pretty close," responded Herman

The following week Herman returned to the spot where he and Betty had observed the accident and directed the Navy divers to where the plane had gone in, but they found nothing. The deep mud had swallowed up all trace of the aircraft. Recovery operations were called off and the divers returned to their base in Seattle.

After suffering the loss of four planes within a month, the

Navy suspended military operations on the Clear Lake bombing range and the Goose Lake gunnery range. The Devil's Garden returned to the place it had always been; where sagebrush flats lay tranquil under a breathless, sun-slapped sky; where snow fell and drifted; where the wind brought distinct voices of coyote families; where time had little meaning and the soft, tranquil notes of isolation and solitude came as a welcome relief to Herman and Betty.

TEN

Spring and summer, calving and haying, came and went. The crispness of early autumn was in the air as Ray rode through sage already bleached aqua and gray. The north wind puffed now and then, swirling the white alkali and shaking the sparse and brittle summer grasses. The sun, the color of a dandelion blossom, seemed distant and inconsequential. Far off on the western horizon the Cascade mountains hung suspended in a low purple haze.

Ray topped the rounded spine of the ridge and pulled his horse up near a twisted juniper. In front of him Steele Swamp gleamed like a lovely emerald. He could see the barn and the house and thought he could make out three figures moving around in what remained of the garden. He squinted and saw one of them pushing a wheelbarrow. He figured that was Herman. Betty must be there, too, and the third figure was more than likely Betty's mother, up for a visit before winter locked the ranch in its snowy grasp. Ray liked Leona. He thought that if his brother had to have a mother-in-law, Leona was way better than most.

Shifting his weight Ray swung out of the saddle. He stood on the ground and took a step to shake loose a cramp in one leg, lifted his arms over his head, let them fall and with a sigh leaned back against the juniper. His thoughts wandered to the last time he had been at Steele Swamp. It had been summer. Haying season. The garden was in all its glory, showing cultivated explosions of green tomatoes, beets, peas, corn, potatoes.

Ray recalled one evening in particular. The sun was nearly down but the day held its heat. Betty was tending the garden, straddling the manicured rows, pant legs rolled to her knees, ankle deep in the furrows filled with water. She was bent at the waist and her blouse was pulled taut across her back. She was weeding, working hard, but at length she straightened to stretch the tightness in her back and absently she drew a forearm, hand muddied to her wrist, across her brow. She saw Ray then, waved enthusiastically and flashed him a smile. And Ray knew that he could never love her more than he did at that moment. She was so pretty and genuine. A stab of loneliness, a sharper pain than he had ever felt before, hit him and he told himself that his brother was a very lucky man to have a woman like Betty.

Ray mounted and worked his way off the ridge as the sun set and shadows melted into evening. He met Herman at the barn and they visited on the way to the house.

"We've got company," said Herman.

"I saw. Leona?"

"Naw. You remember me telling you about Betty's friend, Merle Bardt? They were living together in an apartment when I went down to Santa Cruz. She was with us when we got married." Ray nodded. "She's here. Kind of had a tough go the last couple years. She's got a little boy. He's staying with Merle's mother down in California. Merle's fixing to get a divorce. I didn't ask the particulars. Don't care to know. She's been here three days.

Probably stay until she gets a hankering to go home. Shouldn't take long. She's a city gal, claims she needs to be around people. Said she doesn't know how we stand it way out here. Betty and I wouldn't have it any other way. We hate town. Give me this ranch, a good horse and a few cows and I'm content as a hog in a barrel of mash. Yes sir."

The kitchen was warm from the residue of the afternoon sun and made hotter by the fire in the wood stove and a cauldron of steaming water. Colorful jars, filled with the remnants of the garden, lined the counter and spilled onto the table and the floor. Betty and Merle were sitting outside drinking sun tea and waiting for the last round of tin lids to pop and seal. Their hair was piled on top of their heads and wrapped in scarves. Both had on sleeveless blouses.

Betty spotted Ray through the screen door. She jumped to her feet, cocked one hand on her hip and the other behind her head in a glamour pose. "You caught me at my finest. If I knew you were coming I would have put on my Sunday best and baked you a cake."

"And it probably would have been as tough as that pancake you tried to feed me," grinned Ray.

Betty laughed at the memory and hugged Ray, took him by the arm and pulled him forward. She introduced him to Merle. Merle extended her hand. Ray hardly looked up. "Pleased to meet you." They shook hands.

Over the next few days a friendship developed between the quiet Ray and outgoing Merle. They went for walks after supper. Merle told him the intimate details of her failed marriage and her ambivalence about the direction of her life now that her divorce was within days of being finalized. The more time Merle spent with Ray the more she found herself falling for him. She could not understand exactly why. She supposed it was a lot of little things; his shyness, the cute way his hair jutted out from under his cowboy hat as unruly as a raven's wing, the jangle of his rowels. Ray was a man who worked hard and slept soundly. He had strength of character. He was predictable, steady, easy-going. There would be no surprises with a man like Ray. He could be counted on, trusted. He would always be there for her. She thought Ray was absolutely adorable.

Ray led a free and easy life. He owned his tack and saddle and a duffel bag into which was stuffed all the clothes he needed to carry him through four seasons. Ray embodied a spirit as wild as the wind. Merle might have felt challenged to see if she was woman enough to tame that wild spirit. Or was it that Ray happened to be the only available man within a hundred miles? If she had been honest with herself, the true reason she wanted Ray was because of Betty. Betty was happy and content. She shared true romantic love with Herman. Merle wanted the same for herself. And since she could not have Herman, she chose Ray and began to pursue him with small flirtations that, singly, amounted to very little, but cumulatively had the desired effect. Ray was drawn into her web.

Betty and Herman noticed the budding romance and late at night they whispered back and forth in bed about what was transpiring. Betty said it would never work, that Merle was not the kind of girl who would ever be satisfied living on a ranch, miles from town. Merle had some college, she had been married, had a son. She had never lived without electricity, never been snowbound, never in her life had to roll up her sleeves and work. Betty said that if Merle and Ray got together it would be a terrible mistake for both of them. Herman agreed.

"Tell him so," urged Betty. "Talk some sense into him before it's too late."

"It's not my place," whispered Herman. "He'll make up his own mind."

"But don't you think...."

"No," said Herman. The discussion was over. But for a long time Herman lay with his head on the pillow and his eyes open in the dark. He tried to picture Ray and Merle married, the little boy living with them. They would lead a compromised life, probably live on a small farm down in the valley where the marsh had been reclaimed and opened to homesteaders; a place where Ray would be confined to the rigid squares of cropland, where precious water would be squeezed through a series of head gates and flushed through a grid of ditches before being coaxed onto the fields. A landscape of domestication and civilization. A bleak and confining prison for Ray. He would constantly be looking beyond the sea of manufactured green to where stunted sage and rocky outcroppings led a wandering mind into the heart of the Devil's Garden.

As Herman lay there, every once in a while he heard subdued voices or Merle's airy giggle. Ray might think he could be a husband to Merle and a father to her son, but Herman knew better. He was sure he knew Ray better than Ray knew himself.

Several days passed and then one morning Ray said to Herman, "I asked Merle to marry me."

For once Herman found himself at a loss for words. Finally he asked, "What'd she say?"

"Said she would."

Herman, not able to muster much enthusiasm, said, "Hope it all works out. When are you thinking of doing it?"

"Thought maybe we'd run down to Reno today, 'less you have some objection."

Herman shook his head.

Shortly after noon Ray and Merle drove away. Three days later Ray returned. Merle was not with him. When Betty saw Ray's crestfallen face she knew better than to say much more than, "It didn't work out, I guess?"

Ray shook his head. "Guess not."

Later Herman and Ray went for a ride under the pretense of looking over the cattle. When they were as far away from the house as they would get, Ray got off his horse. He squinted into the whorl of shadows thrown off by a juniper, squatted on his haunches and used a stick to gouge at the moist soil. "It wasn't ever going to work, Merle and me."

"She's a nice gal," said Herman. "But you know I have to agree with you. She's different."

"You got Betty," said Ray. He threw the stick away and stood. "I don't have nobody."

As Ray stepped into the stirrup Herman said, "Yeah you do, you've got me and Betty."

Ray's heart was having difficulty clenching and unclenching. His eyes misted. He told himself maybe that was all the love he needed and silently vowed to never again allow a woman to hurt him like Merle had.

"Know what we should do?" said Herman.

"What?"

"Run wild horses," said Herman.

Ray grinned. "When do we leave?"

"How about in the morning?"

"Fine."

Ever since coming to work for Mr. Dalton on the Pitchfork Ranch, Herman and Ray spent a few weeks each year running mustangs. That was their vacation. A time to be unchained from their normal duties and responsibilities, a time to be carefree, reckless and wild.

They rose well before dawn and rode south in the dark. Their saddle horses picked their way through the rocks and the sagebrush while high overhead the Milky Way shimmered in iridescent colors against the black sky.

As they approached Boles Creek, morning birds began to welcome a faint suggestion of daylight. The horses drank and Herman and Ray continued on diverging paths; Ray toward the valley floor and Herman climbing into the hills.

As Herman ascended he could feel a growing sense of anticipation. They were on the range that held the finest wild horses, whose lineage could be traced to California Red, the stallion that had so impressed Zane Grey. California Red's offspring were consistently sound and well-muscled. They were fast, nimble on their feet, easy to break and dependable to ride. No other blood line had as much heart as the mustangs of Pothole Valley. There was no quit in them.

Herman was riding a Pothole Valley mustang named Pepper. As he rode Herman recalled the day he dropped a loop over Pepper's neck. He had been riding with Ray and Ed Donavan. Off in the distance they spotted four colts. From the looks of them they were two-year-olds that the herd stallion had probably kicked out to fend for themselves. There was one horse in particular that caught Herman's attention. He had a gray mane and tail and a black body. Herman said, "I want the one that looks like salt and pepper."

"Me, too," said Ray.

"The one to catch him, gets him," responded Ed as he dug in his spurs. During the chase Herman's horse, Trigger, pulled up lame. Herman thought he had thrown a shoe and muttered, "Doggone it," under his breath and turned around, heading toward home.

After a while Trigger quit limping and Herman thought about returning to the roundup, but he was not convinced Trigger was cured. He eased around a little butte and as they came into the open, out on the flat, he saw three horses running toward him. The horse in the middle was the stud marked like salt and pepper. They had been running for a while and were lathered and spent. Herman pulled Trigger behind a juniper and waited. He allowed the first horse to pass and when the salt and pepper horse came into view he spurred Trigger forward and tossed his loop. It dropped neatly around the head of the colt. Herman went to take his dally but when the colt hit the end of the rope he exploded. He squalled and bawled and made a tight circle around the juniper, breaking off branches as he went. Herman had been riding Trigger all day and the cinch was not as tight as it should have been. The saddle slipped sideways. Herman had two choices; hang on and roll the saddle or let go of his rope. He let go and bailed off. Luckily Trigger ran a short distance and stopped. Herman was able to reset the saddle but by then the colt was long gone, along with Herman's lariat.

As Herman neared home he spotted the colt once again. He was making a big circle, kicking at the rope that trailed behind raising dust and occasionally slapping him on his rump or side. Herman kicked Trigger into a hard gallop. They overtook the colt near the field where thirty head of horses were pastured and drove him through the four-wire fence, hitting so hard the wires popped. The colt never got a scratch.

Herman repaired the fence, opened the gate and ran all the horses into the corral. He separated out the colt, retrieved his lariat and turned the other horses back into the pasture.

Ray and Ed came in late that afternoon complaining that Herman, leaving like he did, had ruined the roundup. They accused Herman of returning so he could lie around the house.

"Come with me." Herman led the way to the corral. The sleek colt was pacing back and forth. "I've decided to call him Pepper."

"How'd you manage that?" Ed asked in bewilderment.

"He was waiting here for me when I came in." Herman would say no more.

The next morning they roped the colt and cut him. A few days later Herman began breaking the gelding and in time Pepper became a dappled gray and one of the best ranch horses in the country.

Now Herman patted Pepper's neck and looked off in the direction from where Ray would be pushing the wild horses. It seemed as though the only life on the landscape was a gathering wind and the red-tailed hawk that perched in the top of a nearby snag. His breast feathers flushed and relaxed in the gusting wind. His head swivelled and yellow eyes flashed as he hoped to catch sight of an anxious rodent on a last-minute errand before the arrival of the coming storm. His talons released, wings unfolded and he rode the wind south.

Somewhere down below was a band of wild horses. Probably hunkered down in a swale out of this wind. Sorrel, pinto, bay, black, smoke, grullo; a shaggy puzzle of colors standing close together to share their heat. The colts and fillies would be to the inside, their breaths mingling.

The wind was growing colder by the minute and Herman flipped up the collar of his coat, tugged at his hat and adjusted the brim low over his eyes. He tucked his lariat under one arm, put his hands together and blew into the pocket of his fingers. When he looked again the hillside was just as desolate as he remembered, splotched with rocks and sage, as blue-gray as gunmetal. And then, above the howl of the wind, he felt a slight vibration.

Pepper's ears twitched and he turned his head toward the sound of the rhythmic drumming of horses' hooves striking against the skin of the calloused ground. Herman shifted his weight to the balls of his feet in the stirrups. He unlimbered his lariat and shook loose a loop. Pepper tossed his head and snorted. Herman watched between the juniper's branches and spotted horses on the move, angling over the rise that funneled toward the narrow opening where he was hiding. Herman allowed two horses to pass. The third was a fine palomino colt. Herman dug his spurs into Pepper's ribs. Pepper responded.

By the time Ray arrived on the scene the palomino was roped and snubbed up tight against Pepper. Ray hollered, "Herman, there's another just like him, over the hill, wanting to come this way. Quick, let's throw this one and try for two."

The Vowell brothers pulled it off. They captured both palominos and as the first storm of the season began spitting snow they trailed the wild horses toward home. As they reached the corrals, snow began to accumulate in a layer that covered the imperfections of the land. Ray felt good. Not once during that long day had his thoughts drifted to Merle.

ELEVEN

With the surrender of Japan local soldiers began to drift home to the Klamath Basin. Friends and buckaroos who had ridden with Herman and Ray dropped in at Steele Swamp for a visit. Some stayed a night or two, others prolonged their visit for a month or more.

Bud Fairclo was one of the Northwest's most decorated soldiers; he received the Distinguished Service Cross for exceptional heroism in combat as well as a Purple Heart, a combat infantry badge, the American Defense Ribbon and the Italian War Cross of Valor. When he arrived at Steele Swamp Bud was suffering from the effects of shell shock and battle fatigue. He could not raise a cup of coffee to his mouth without the contents slopping over the sides. He never spoke of the war and his overseas experiences. All he wanted was to ride and be alone. Gradually he started helping Herman and Ray, working cattle and chasing and breaking wild horses. Time, open space and hard work proved to be an effective antidote for his frayed nerves.

In the evenings Herman, Ray and Bud sat and reminisced. Sometimes Betty joined them but more often than not she found something to do while the men talked. One evening the conversation turned to a mutual friend, Tarzan Dodson. Bud wondered, "What ever happened to Tarzan?"

"Last I heard he was on the SX," said Herman. "You remember Les Morgan, don't you?"

"Sure," said Bud. "He drank whenever he had the price of a beer or, for that matter, whenever he could find someone to buy him a beer. Great guy."

"Yep, that's for sure, you bet ya," offered Ray.

Herman continued, "This one time, it was during haying, Les was driving a wagon. Tarzan came riding up on a colt he was breaking. Les told him to ride with him for a spell so they could visit. Tarzan got off and put his reins through the ring on back of the wagon. He doubled the reins and was pushing them through when the work horses jumped ahead. Tarzan finished tying his horse and as he climbed onto the seat he made a passing comment to Les, saying that goosing his team thataway was gonna cost him a beer 'cause it made him lose his thumb. Les looked and sure enough Tarzan wasn't kidding. When the horses jumped ahead his thumb got caught in the loop. It popped off at the first joint as slick as calf slobbers."

"What'd Les do?" Bud wanted to know.

Ray snickered, "Bought him a beer." They laughed.

"Another Tarzan and Les story. Seems the two of them were in a bar down in Alturas. A drunk had passed out and Tarzan claimed he was dead. So he and Les packed the drunk out behind the old hotel. They located a couple shovels and proceeded to dig a grave. They laid the fellow in the hole, tossed on a few shovels of dirt, lost interest and went back to the bar for a drink. According to the fellow who told me, when the drunk came to, he found himself in the grave with dirt piled on his chest. He sobered up in a hurry, swore off drinking and, to this day, hasn't touched a drop of alcohol."

Bud did not laugh like he was supposed to. Maybe it was the mention of being dead or digging a grave but something tripped a trigger in his psyche. After a moment he began talking. "I've seen more death than any one man should ever have to see." He waited another long moment. "I was in North Africa, we came up the coast to Tunis fighting every step of the way, crossed the Mediterranean on troop ships and fought our way into Sicily. One place we were 63 days lying in the mud and never had a bath in all that time. We used to throw cigarettes back and forth with the Germans. We were that close."

Betty poured more coffee and sat with the men. She said, "We read in the newspaper they gave you the Distinguished Service Cross."

"Yep," said Bud.

"Where were you?" asked Betty, hoping that Bud would continue talking. She thought he needed to get what happened out in the open.

"We were trying to take a mountain top near Cassino, Italy. I came across a pillbox, snuck up and captured four Germans. I took them behind our lines, turned around and started back up the hill. But the Germans counter-attacked. Off to my left a machine gun opened fire and I hit the ground, crawled on my belly, lobbed a grenade in and killed every man inside. But I gave away my position. The Germans concentrated their fire on me. I took a slug in this wrist, got the scar to prove it, right here, and it knocked my rifle out of my hand. My only salvation was to take cover in the pillbox. Bullets were flying, ricocheting around me like corn popping in a fry pan."

"Weren't you scared?" asked Betty.

"Scared as hell. I crouched in a corner, pulled my helmet over my head and held onto a little Bible I was carrying. I prayed. Prayed like I never prayed in my life. Promised the Lord if He let me live I'd get baptized. That night, huddled in the German pillbox, was the longest night of my life.

"When it started to get light I heard movement outside and figured it had to be Germans. A voice called, said to come out or they were going to blow me out. It was an American. I hollered my name and outfit and they came in and got me.

"I was sent to a field hospital. The bad part was the Army messed up, listed me killed in action and sent a telegram to that effect to my folks. They thought I was dead until the letter I wrote from the hospital, saying I had been wounded but was healing fast, arrived.

"The medals and all that stuff, the glory, I never went looking for any of it. When someone is shooting at you, you don't have time to think. You react. Try to stay alive. Basic survival."

"Did you get baptized?" Betty wanted to know.

"I keep my promises."

"Ray and I wish we would have gone in."

"You didn't miss nothin'," said Bud.

"When I got back from California, right after Pearl Harbor, Ray and I stayed up all night and talked about things. We decided to enlist. But when we told Mr. Dalton he asked us to reconsider. He said if he was going to keep the ranch operating he couldn't spare either one of us, and that if we stuck with him he would speak to the draft board on our behalf and see if he could get us reclassified. I told him not to. It didn't sound fair to me. The way we left it was Ray and I would wait and if we got our draft notice then we would go. Mr. Dalton knew that if it ever came to the point in the fighting where we felt as though we were absolutely needed, nothing could have stopped us from joining up and going to war."

"We took our physicals and passed," said Ray.

"Once we got our 1-A classification cards I really thought we would be called up," said Herman. "I was so sure I spoke with Mr. Dalton, told him while I was gone I didn't want anybody riding Pepper. Didn't want him spoiled. But what would have bothered me most was Betty, what to do with her. Once we got married I knew she couldn't stay here."

"I was going to move back to California and live with my folks. As soon as Herman got stationed somewhere I planned on joining him, at least until he was shipped overseas," said Betty. "That was our plan. It would have been tough, not having Herman, not being here, not having a horse to ride."

"We stayed 1-A throughout the war. I think what happened was Mr. Dalton pulled a few strings; talked to the draft board and told them he couldn't run the outfit without us. He wanted to keep us that bad," said Herman.

"Never short-change yourselves. You were vitally important to the war effort," said Bud.

"I still don't feel quite right," said Herman. "It was like we didn't contribute as much as you fighting men."

"To win the war it took men in the trenches and everyone at home supporting us. You were as much a part of that team as I was. We had to eat. You provided food," said Bud. "You want to know what kept me going when we were slogging through the mud and it looked like the war was never going to end? I remembered times with the two of you; chasing wild horses, rounding up cattle, riding the range, breaking colts, bucking broncs at the rodeo. That's what kept me going. The thought of getting back here gave me a reason to live. I was damn lucky. And here I am."

Talking about the war seemed to help Bud and in the days ahead his shaking became less noticeable. He was able to sleep through the night, although he still occasionally shouted himself awake or woke suddenly in a cold sweat. One morning at breakfast he announced he was going to drive to Dairy, his hometown, and visit his folks. He said he might spend a few days looking up old friends.

During this time he attended a dance and became reacquainted with a girl he had known before the war. Bud and Erma Rogers began dating and soon married. They bought a small ranch along the state line south of Malin. From their place it was 24 miles across the Devil's Garden to Steele Swamp. Bud and Erma spent much of their spare time with Herman and Betty. As a foursome they threw horse shoes, rode horses and roped calves. One of the things they enjoyed most was attending rodeos. Bud rode an occasional bronc, but Herman and Ray entered nearly every event; from the cowboy foot race to wild cow milking, saddle bronc to roping events. They participated in cutting horse and reining cow horse competitions, riding horses they had captured as wild mustangs and trained themselves.

The Vowell brothers were rodeo heroes to almost everyone in the basin country. They were living legends and won or placed high in the rough stock events and claimed nearly every roping event; steer roping, calf roping and team roping. They had spent so much time riding and working together that in an arena they knew what the other would do before he did it. Betty got in on the action, too. She ran barrels and at Cedarville she and Herman received a trophy for the best looking couple in the parade. Herman won the All-Around Cowboy at Lakeview. Ray was the Modoc County All-Around Champion. The two of them went back and forth winning events and All-Around titles. They were competitive in a friendly, good-natured way, rooting for each other but always letting the other know when one proved to be the better man on a particular day.

At the Cedarville Rodeo Herman managed to go one up on Ray. On that day a fellow got to drinking and fighting. He outran the sheriff and, in an effort to escape, tried to run across the arena. Herman was warming up for calf-roping, saw what was happening and urged his horse into motion. He roped the man and, to the cheers of the crowd, would have hogtied him if the sheriff had not caught up to the action and made his arrest. Herman received headlines in the newspaper.

When Erma Fairclo heard the Forest Service was looking for someone to work at the lookout on Blue Mountain, she immediately thought of her good friend Rachel Gysbers. Rachel was a native of Klamath Falls and trained as an Army nurse. After the war she returned home and found work with a local doctor, but the doctor suffered a stroke and was forced to take the summer off from his practice.

"It would be perfect," Erma told Rachel. "I think you would really enjoy the experience. They're giving preference points to anyone who was in the service so you should have the inside track. And if you get the job we'll be neighbors, close enough to visit."

What Erma failed to mention was that Blue Mountain was only nine miles from Steele Swamp and she was playing cupid. She thought Rachel would be the perfect mate for Ray.

One Sunday Erma drove Rachel to Steele Swamp to meet the Vowells. On the way back Erma asked Rachel, who was nearly thirty years old and had never married, her impression of the Vowells.

"It was strange," said Rachel. "I know I just met them but it seems as though I have known them all my life. They certainly are nice folks. And Betty is a double dandy, personality and so pretty. I just loved her."

"And Herman?"

"One of a kind, isn't he," laughed Rachel. "Full of stories and jokes. Not a dull moment when he's around."

"You're right about that," said Erma. She pressed on, "And what about Ray?"

"A lot more quiet," said Rachel, "but I suppose around Herman he doesn't have much of a choice." What Rachel did not mention was that she had taken a shine to Ray. He was a gentleman. He was quiet, serious, respectful and more than a little shy. Although he was not a church goer he had confided he read his Bible nearly every evening. Rachel could clearly see he was at peace spiritually, and in her thinking he was one of those rare individuals who was completely comfortable with himself. All of these were qualities that Rachel admired in a man. She wanted to see more of Ray and if a romance between them developed she would welcome it.

Rachel got the job. Her father, who had taken her camping when she was young and was responsible for instilling in her a love of the outdoors, drove her to Blue Mountain. The lookout was a glass house built on stilts, perched on the 5,740-foot summit. From the exposed vantage Rachel could see from the Warner Mountains to the Cascades, north into Oregon and south to Mount Shasta. Below the ridge stretched the Devil's Garden and Rachel was excited to discover she could look into Steele Swamp, although the house and barn were hidden from her view.

Rachel's father departed and for the longest time Rachel watched the dust trail he made going down the mountain and across the flat. She had never felt so free in her life. A forked-horned mule deer, still in velvet, came and grazed in the opening under the lookout. A hawk hovered on the wind. Rachel got out her bird identification book and searched through the illustrations before deciding, based on the light-colored tail crossed by a broad black band, that the bird was most likely a rough-legged hawk. The sun set and each fir along the skyline threw a perfect triangular shadow to the east. The stars came out. Rachel fell asleep surrounded by the absolute quiet of the isolated mountain. In the morning the sun emerged, the night chill dropped away and the birds sang and preened and skittered in the topmost limbs of the pines. Rachel watched the sun ratchet upward into a blue sky and the shadows shrink as a line of light marched across Steele Swamp. She imagined Ray traipsing toward the barn to begin morning chores.

The heat of the day swelled and tar black butterflies flitted around the windows. Rachel watched sunlight dance on the aspen trees tucked into a watered draw, their leaves quaked from silver to apple-green in a slight breeze. The breeze brought the fragrance of yellow buttercups, bursts of wild lavender, the weedy scent of Indian paintbrush and, from the flats below, the unmistakable tang of sage. Rachel left her lofty perch and climbed around on the boulders at the base of the tower. The soles of her shoes scuffed against the scaly reddish-brown and corn-yellow lichens that covered them. Soon she scurried back to the lookout. Every fifteen minutes she was required to survey the country with field glasses and search for any signs of smoke. She scanned in all directions. Her gaze always lingered on Steele Swamp.

After a few days Rachel realized she might be alone on the lookout but she was far from isolated. She had a telephone and in the evenings frequently called Betty to visit. She knew there was no privacy and everyone on the party line was probably listening. Betty had also counseled her about proper party line etiquette; listeners were not to breathe heavily or to have a radio playing in the background. It was acceptable to listen in on conversations but not permissible to join in with a comment.

Betty told Rachel about the time Herman called the home ranch to phone in a lumber order. He said he needed so many two-by-fours this length and so many that length, and some two-by-sixes, and on and on. Mr. Dalton was having a difficult time understanding exactly what was needed. Suddenly a deep voice came on the line and said, "Mr. Dalton, Herman says he needs...."

The more people who listened in, the weaker the signal became. Betty told Rachel one time she was trying to talk to Thelma Archer at Willow Creek and the connection was so bad she finally said into the receiver, "If a couple of you will hang up so I can hear Thelma, I promise to call you back and let you know what was said." There were several laughs followed by quick clicks as receivers were returned to their cradles.

Rachel learned that each user had a different ring and that Steel Swamp was two longs and two shorts. The phone proved to be an amusing way to stay in contact with people and Rachel soon came to know the detailed lives of people she had never met. Betty had told her that in the winter there were only two ranches on the party line, Steele Swamp and Willow Creek, and that she and Thelma Archer would play cribbage over the phone. They each had boards and played with two decks. One time Herman advised Betty not to play because if Thelma thought Betty was cheating, or Betty thought Thelma was cheating, it could end their friendship. Betty was so angry she refused to talk to Herman for several hours, and when she did she told him he would never be able to understand women, or their level of mutual trust. Before they went to bed, according to a promise they had made when they married, they kissed and made up.

Once a week Rachel called the Forest Service headquarters in Alturas and gave them a list of groceries. They were delivered along with three five-gallon cans of water. Every few weeks a Forest Service employee would offer to spend the night at the tower and on those occasions Rachel called Steele Swamp and either Herman or Ray would drive to the lookout and bring Rachel to the ranch.

August 12 was cool and rainy. Rachel looked at her calendar, realized it was Betty and Herman's wedding anniversary, and decided to bake them a chocolate cake. Even at her best Rachel was a so-so cook but she made a special effort. Her mistake was opening the oven door before the cake had finished baking. The center fell but Rachel frosted it anyway.

The rain continued and Rachel called Forest Service headquarters and asked permission to leave the lookout. There was no chance of a fire breaking out and her request was granted. Rachel started down the mountain. She walked nine miles to Steele Swamp and presented the anniversary cake to Betty, who acted as though it were the finest gift she had ever received.

That evening Betty planned to cook T-bone steaks. Ray liked his steak rare and no matter how short of a time Betty cooked his steak, Ray always complained it was not quite rare enough to suit his taste. Betty confided to Rachel, "I'll make Ray's steak rare enough for him tonight, just watch me." She cooked all the steaks but one and with the skillet red hot she threw Ray's steak on only long enough to sear the surface, then she flipped it and did the same to the other side.

Ray cut the first bite and red blood ran in rivulets. With an evil glint in her eye Betty asked him, "How's your steak, Ray? Rare enough for you?"

"Just right," said Ray. He ate every bite.

For dessert Betty served Rachel's cake and from the way Herman and Ray carried on Rachel got the impression that even Betty had never made a better tasting dessert.

The following morning Herman drove Rachel to the lookout. On the way Rachel said, "Herman, I'm so happy you and Betty found each other. The two of you are a perfect match. Your marriage must have been made in heaven."

Later that summer Herman made a quick trip to town for parts and when he got to the parts store he found a poem Betty had written him. It read:

> *When you drove off we kissed goodbye,*
> *you took the warmth from a sunlit sky.*
> *You took the glow from a happy heart,*
> *it is so sad while we're apart.*
> *We were meant to be one, not be two,*
> *and, oh my darling, I am lonesome for you.*
> *Hours drag by and the day will be long,*
> *minutes are endless while you are gone.*
> *Don't you know you're the light of my life,*
> *please hurry home to your lonely wife.*
> *Betty*

On the return trip the pickup quit running. Herman started walking but after a couple miles his cowboy boots had worn blisters on his heels and toes. He came to a spring where cattle were gathered and as he neared they moved away, kicking up dust as they went. This gave Herman an idea. He would scare the cattle, making them run and stir up a dust cloud. Rachel would surely notice this, check it out with her binoculars, see Herman waving his arms and call the ranch and let them know he needed a ride.

Rachel had no problem seeing the cloud of dust from the stampeding cattle. In fact, when Herman ran them off he did such a dandy job that the dust cloud completely obscured him. Herman had to walk six more miles to reach home. When he got there he called Rachel and chided her about her inability to spot a real emergency.

The fire season ended and Rachel returned to Klamath Falls and her work with the doctor. When Ray had a free weekend he would sometimes call her and they would go to dinner and a movie. He liked westerns. At the end of the evening he thanked her and gave her a goodnight peck on the cheek. Their relationship never progressed beyond the friendship stage. Rachel never told Ray she had feelings for him.

In the back of her mind Rachel always figured Ray compared her to Betty. Rachel felt such a comparison was completely unfair. Betty was an expert rider and she could rope and work cows with the best buckaroos. She was a wonderful cook, a perfect wife and no matter whether she was canning or branding she was able to maintain an aura of personal beauty. There was no woman alive who could compare favorably to Betty. She was one of a kind, a precious diamond of perfection. Rachel could have been jealous, but she was not. Instead, she was extremely honored to be able to call Betty her best friend.

When Betty suffered her tubal pregnancy in March 1948 and was saved with the dramatic emergency operation in the kitchen, it was their close friendship that prompted Rachel to volunteer her services as a registered nurse. Bud Arnold flew her to Steele

Swamp.

The fourth day after the operation Billy Dalton ferried Leona to the ranch in a four-wheel drive jeep. By then Betty was well on the road to recovery. She was eating and able to get out of bed and walk with some assistance. Rachel elected to come out with Billy.

During her stay at the ranch Rachel and Ray had spent a lot of time together and in the following months Rachel thought Ray just might ask her to marry him. But he never did. And finally she gave up on him. One night, after dinner and a movie in Klamath Falls, Rachel told Ray she had been offered a job in Alaska. She was hoping he might try to talk her out of going. Instead Ray told her, "Well, I guess this is goodby. Be sure and write."

And that was the end of it.

TWELVE

The summer of 1950 Ray and a family friend, Jimmy Farrel, were buckarooing near Clear Lake. It had been one of the driest years on record and the lake was lower than anyone could recall. The two men were taking a shortcut across an exposed elbow of the lake when they happened upon two skeletons.

"I'll bet those are the flyboys who went in," said Ray.

"When was that?" Jimmy wanted to know.

Ray sat on his horse, one forearm resting on the saddle horn, staring at the skeletons. He squinted, said, "Late in '44. Herman and Betty saw it from that ridge over yonder. Saw the whole thing."

"What happened?"

"Torpedo bomber. Went into a dive. Never pulled out."

"Guess we better notify the authorities," said Jimmy.

"Yep." When Ray arrived at Steele Swamp he called the

sheriff and reported the finding, saying he thought he had located the two Navy men who crashed into Clear Lake, they were skeletons but pretty well preserved.

"Can you find them again?" asked the sheriff.

"Sure, take you right there."

The sheriff collected the skeletons and sent the skulls to the University of California for identification. The results confirmed the remains were definitely Indian. When a story was printed in the newspaper it stated Clear Lake had been an Indian burial ground and people flocked to the area to hunt for exposed artifacts. The scavengers collected mortars and pestles, arrowheads, spear points and human remains.

A few weeks later Ray, Jimmy, Herman and Betty were gathering cattle near Clear Lake. When they came to the place where the skeletons had been found Ray pointed out the spot. Nearby someone had lined up several dozen Indian skulls, placed them in a row, and used them for target practice.

"That is disgusting," said Betty. "Why do that?"

"I don't know," responded Herman with a sad shake of his head.

They stopped for lunch on the sagebrush hill overlooking Fiddler's Green. They passed Zane Grey's cabin at Mammoth Spring and pushed the cattle along the route of the old emigrant trail. As they neared the fence surrounding Steele Swamp, Jimmy went ahead to open the gate.

Betty was riding a big palomino named Thunderhead, a good circle horse that could go in a thirty-mile loop and finish the day just as strong as he started it. Normally he was gentle and dependable.

The afternoon was hot and Betty breathed in the stale odor of Thunderhead's sweat along with the sun-baked soil and the smell of cattle. The country here had been reduced to simple dichromatic shades of sagebrush gray and the verdant green of the pasture. The summer sky swelled with cumulus clouds as moisture-laden air off the Pacific overran the heat of the high desert.

The palomino knew they were getting close to the end of the drive and was anxious to reach the corral and have his saddle removed so he could roll in the dust, shake himself and mill around with the other horses until they were rewarded with rolled oats, payment for a day's work. The cattle were not lining out and flowing through the gate as they should. One cow butted another and she side-stepped and pushed into Thunderhead. He moved to get out of the way and when he did a hind foot came in contact with a hunk of wire. He kicked at it. A wire loop flipped up, wrapped around his foot, came tight. Thunderhead rolled his eyes until nothing but white showed. Ears twitched. Tail came up and he humped his back like a Halloween cat.

Herman was no more than 30 feet away and saw everything as it transpired but there was nothing he could do. He started to holler. The words never came out of his mouth. Thunderhead rose off the ground, all four feet, twisting his body, grunting, kicking with his hind legs. His front legs hit the ground first, hit with a wickedly sharp jolt.

Betty had no warning. There was no time for her to prepare herself or react. One moment she was concentrating on one cow butting another, then she might have been aware of a flick of a hind foot as Thunderhead shifted his weight, the quiver that ran the length of his spine, the hump of his back. In the aftermath of the unexpected explosion Betty was tossed over the forks of the saddle and, still clutching the reins, made a smooth arc that ended with her being slammed, face-first, into a pile of rocks.

Fear instantly tightened the flesh on Herman's face. He did not want to be a part of this terrible ordeal, not right now, not ever. He had almost lost Betty once, he did not think he could face a similar tragedy. A voice within beseeched him to spin his horse, ride flat out toward the gradual curve of the earth, digging with his spurs, allowing the wind and the speed to calm him, finding reassurance in the familiar skip of the hooves as feet lightly touched down, lifted off, touched down, lifted off....

A humph of air escaped from Herman, as though he had

been punched in the solar plexus, and in spite of his inner struggles he urged his horse to where Betty lay crumpled against the rocks. He leaped down, dropped to his knees, reached toward Betty but pulled his hands away and shouted to Jimmy. "Get to the ranch as fast as you can. Bring the pickup. Throw a mattress in. Move."

Ray continued to ride, keeping the cattle away while Herman turned his attention back to Betty. He placed his hands on her shoulders and gently, slowly, lifted her. She reminded him of a tiny, broken sparrow that had flown into a window. He turned her inward against his chest, cradling her in his arms. It frightened him to see the blood, the open wounds and the terrible damage that had been done to her face. He thought she was dead. Tears stung his eyes but then he saw a tiny bubble of froth appear on her bruised lips. It stretched and shrank to the same cadence echoed by the slight rise and fall of her chest. She was breathing. She was alive. Herman held her in his arms, rocking slightly, crying openly.

Jimmy had eight gates to maneuver through on his wild three-mile ride to ranch headquarters. When he got there he turned his horse loose, fired up the pickup, swung by the bunkhouse, grabbed a mattress and threw it in back. He drove fast, spinning tires, bouncing over rocks and sliding around corners.

When Jimmy arrived Herman was dry-eyed and holding Betty's head and shoulders on his lap. He looked scared. He demanded to know, "What took so long, Jimmy?"

"Came fast as I could."

Herman shifted his legs around and rose with Betty in his arms. He carried her to the pickup where he laid her on the mattress in back. He climbed in and sat beside her. He instructed Jimmy, "Let's get going. Take it easy. Don't jostle her any more than you have to."

Ray led the way on horseback and as the pickup came to a stop under the poplar trees in the yard Herman instructed Jimmy to stay with Betty and hollered to Ray, "Get your car ready to roll. I'm calling Dr. Martin."

Ray had recently bought a new Nash sedan, a big, heavy, powerful car. One of the special features was that the passenger's seat folded all the way down to become a bed. Ray lowered the seat. When Herman came flying from the house with an armload of towels and blankets, Ray called to him. "What'd he say?"

"Get her to town as quick as we can," said Herman. He carried Betty to the car, laid her on the front seat of the Nash and tucked the blankets and towels around her. He climbed in back and held her. Leaving Jimmy behind at the ranch to tend the stock and shut the gates, they sped toward town.

Ray took the long road, 75 miles around through Hackamore, because it was a much better road than the cutoff that skirted Clear Lake. He drove loosely, giving the car its head. They swept through corners as if propelled by a hard wind and a big sail, and on the flats the motor growled and tires chattered the washboard, hitting only the high spots. When they arrived in Malin Herman dashed into Dr. Martin's office. The doctor was with a patient but hurried outside, opened the car door and knelt beside Betty. As he examined her he wanted to know, "Has she vomited?"

Herman said, "No. Why? Is that a bad sign?"

"Very bad," said Dr. Martin. "It would mean a severe brain injury."

He had no sooner spoken those words than Betty began vomiting. Dr. Martin made sure her air passage was open and then he stood and instructed Herman, "Get her to the hospital. I'll telephone you're coming. I'm shutting down the office and will be right behind you."

The Nash squealed to a stop at the emergency door of the Klamath Valley Hospital. Herman commandeered a gurney, wheeled it outside and was transferring Betty to it when several nurses and an orderly showed up and took over. Herman followed them inside and down the hallway but when they came to a double door, one of the nurses took him by the arm.

"We'll take good care of her," said the nurse.

"Can I go in?" pleaded Herman.

"You'd only get in the way."

Ray arrived and fell in step, walking behind Herman and the nurse. Ray dropped down in a chair in the waiting room and put his head in his hands. Herman looked at his watch. Exactly four hours had transpired since the accident.

Time passed slowly, but finally Dr. Martin appeared. His tone was somber, his voice barely audible. "I'm not going to try and sugar coat this, Herman. It's serious. Betty is still unconscious. She has a basal skull fracture and a broken right wrist. I set the wrist. But what concerns us is the swelling of her brain. If it subsides I think she'll have a fighting chance."

Herman's bottom lip trembled. "Can I see her? Can I stay with her?"

"Of course," said Dr. Martin. "Give us a few minutes. I'll have one of the nurses come for you." He turned his attention to Ray. "You can look in, but I really don't want to overdo it. I hope you understand."

"Maybe I'll go back to the ranch, grab Herman a change of clothes," said Ray.

Herman was not thinking clearly. He told Ray, "Take care of my horse. Put him away, will you?"

"Sure. Yeah. You bet," said Ray even though he knew Jimmy already had.

The following morning Betty's face was horribly swollen and discolored. But she was showing signs of regaining consciousness, licking her lips and beneath her closed lids she was moving her eyes. Her lips and tongue were badly distended but she managed to form the words, "Where am I?"

"I'm right here." Herman leaned over her, only a few inches from her battered face, waiting for her to come fully awake. When the bruised lids did flutter open Betty's eyes were grotesquely crossed. Herman had not prepared himself for such a bizarre turn of events and involuntarily took a step backward. Then another and another. He was at the door and pushing it open, calling, "Nurse. Nurse." And when the nurse arrived he said, "She's awake," and then clenching his fists tightly he declared in a violent whisper, "It's her eyes. Her eyes."

Dr. Martin explained to Herman why Betty's eyes had crossed. He said that when the skull fractured, the optic nerve became momentarily pinched. He thought if she were to wear a patch over one eye, and then the other, the eyes might return to their normal position. He said if they failed to correct themselves they could, more than likely, be surgically repaired.

Betty remained in the hospital for nine days and then she stayed in Klamath Falls with Herman and Ray's sister, Ina Addington. Betty faithfully wore an eye patch but the eyes remained crossed. During this time Herman drove back and forth between the ranch and Ina's place to be with Betty. It was not until the 26th of October that he was allowed to take her home.

Over the next year Betty underwent three operations at a hospital in San Francisco. Before the third operation the specialist advised, "Whatever we do this time will be permanent and final. Your eyes might be crossed or you might have double vision, but I'm confident we can give you back your eyesight."

Two days after the operation Dr. Barkan and his surgical team removed the bandages from Betty's eyes. The last wrap came off and Betty blinked several times. Dr. Barkan tested the eyes; they tracked left, they tracked right, they tracked up and down. When he had concluded several more tests he turned to his colleagues and announced, "She has perfect vision." The doctors and nurses applauded. Herman realized just how sensitive the operation had been and what a miracle Dr. Barkan had performed.

"The only thing this patient lacks is muscle strength in the right eye," said Dr. Barkan. "She will experience some difficulty looking to her right."

"Gee, I wish it was the other way around," said Betty.

"Why is that, my dear?" said the doctor.

"When I'm roping and dragging calves to the branding fire I look over my right shoulder."

Laughter broke the tension in the room. Dr. Barkan told Betty, "You will have to make do, young lady."

Herman and Betty returned home. The next day they had a visitor. He was a bearded old man who rode in on a worn-out saddle horse, trailing a pack horse and a loose mare, obviously pregnant. Herman recognized the saddle horse before he recalled the distinctive set of chaps, decorated with brands, that the old man was wearing. "Fred Westfall?"

"Fifteen years'n' I ain't changed one bit," drawled Fred.

Herman responded dryly. "Never said that. My God, you look older than the hills. I wouldn't have known who it was but I recognized the chaps, and the fact you're riding the same horse you left out of here on. I never forget a good horse."

"Sure 'nough am," said Fred with pride. "Tell me somethin', you the head honcho of this here outfit?"

"I am," said Herman. "You remember Ray?" Fred nodded. "He's buckaroo boss."

"Be danged," said Fred.

"Why don't you crawl on down, put that relic you're riding in the corral, turn the others in with her, give them all some grain. Looks like they could sure enough use it. That loose mare, she looks about ready to foal?"

"Mighty perceptive," groused Fred. "Believe I'll ride ta the corral. No sense walkin' farther'n I have ta."

"I'll let Betty know to set an extra plate."

"If it's no problem."

"No problem at all."

"Ya got yurself a woman?"

"Sure do. Prettiest gal in three states."

"Man like you needs someone ta take care of him." With that said, Fred made his way toward the corral.

As soon as Fred walked into her kitchen Betty sized him up; he might have a cranky, disagreeable exterior but he was a good-hearted soul. Over dinner she wanted to know all about where he had been, what he had done, if he really had ridden all the way from Nevada. In Fred's round-about-way he answered all of her questions. He said he had been buckarooing in Nevada ever since he left the cattle drive at Goose Lake in 1936. And he said he had indeed come up from Nevada, riding the same mare he left on.

"Figure I done wore out my welcome down south," he claimed. "They wanted ta demote me ta wrangler, but I wasn't havin' none of it. Last day I let all the buckaroos get outta camp an' then I took a gallon of molasses an' poured it in their bedrolls. First day I rode hard an' fast. Better 'n fifty miles. Thought it best ta put some distance 'tween us. An' here I am."

Fred made a big deal out of the fact his pack mare and the loose mare were daughters from his saddle horse. He bragged the mare due to foal had been bred by an expensive stallion but admitted it was going to be a catch-foal and he was not positive of the father, except he was quite sure it had to be a prize winner.

One morning Fred went to the barn and in the pen with his mare was a long-eared baby mule. Fred was dumbfounded and absolutely disgusted at this strange twist of events. He kept mumbling that he could not understand how such a dastardly thing could have happened to his mare and figured someone had played a practical joke at his expense.

As soon as the foal could travel Fred asked Ray to shoe his saddle horse and the pack horse. He paid with a magnifying glass and a pocket knife and departed for Malin, where he sold the mare and the baby mule to the first buyer who made an offer. After that he took Herman's suggestion and swung by the home ranch. Mr. Dalton hired him as caretaker.

THIRTEEN

The spring of 1952 arrived slowly. On the north side of the hills piles of snow lingered in dirty, thin drifts. On the exposed flats the sun tried to convince the grass to poke its way up through the smear of gray soil.

Early one morning a U.S. Forest Service pickup bumped over the Hackamore Road to a prearranged spot in the heart of the Devil's Garden. Two men were in the government pickup; the older man, Gene, was a local. He had been a ranch hand and had worked as a buckaroo. But ten years earlier the government had enticed him with a steady job, a livable wage and generous benefits. He had taken the easy route and now, as Gene stepped from the pickup into the dawn of early morning, he had the devil to pay. He had no stomach for what he was being required to do. It ate away at his insides.

The other was a kid, barely 21 years old. He had never chased a wild horse over the desert landscape, had never roped a mustang. He hailed from Detroit, Michigan and had come west because he had read every book Zane Grey wrote and was in love with the abstract image of a man challenging himself against the western frontier, or more likely, the myth of the western frontier. The kid was anxious for the killing to begin.

The sun winked over the summit of the Warner Mountains and immediately began to warm the air. A marmot waddled out to take up residence on an exposed boulder. His head swivelled and he bounced up and down on his front legs while emitting a series of high-pitched chirps and whistles. He sat, tail snapped upright and his front teeth flashed orange. The kid had a hankering to shoot the varmint and raised his rifle but Gene stopped him, saying as he nodded toward the valley below, "You'll spook 'em."

Below, where the land leveled off, a long way away, was a small band of wild horses. They milled around, nickering softly, communicating with each other. Their winter coats were shaggy, shedding in uneven patches and snarled with dried weeds and sticktights. The stud horse, a black with a mane and tail the color of smoke, nudged his favorite mare, a rangy bay whose legs ran white from her knees down. She had a classy black colt at her side.

Gene watched them through binoculars and slowly, but with the surety of a badger clawing its way out of hibernation, a knot of panic rose within his chest. To steady himself he laid the binoculars on the hood of the pickup and pulled on a pair of work gloves, seating the leather precisely between each finger. He kicked at a small rock. His boots were the same dusty brown as the soil. He pulled his .30-30 carbine from its riding scabbard and could feel the blued barrel through the layer of gloved leather. It was as cool as the linoleum had been early that morning when he had swung his legs out of bed and sat with his feet touching the cool floor. He had dressed in the dark, fixed a pot of coffee, filled his thermos and headed for the door. On the way he retrieved his rifle from the gun cabinet, as well as several boxes of shells. At the hat rack he took a Stetson silver-belly, free from sweat stain and manure, and set it on his head as he opened the door and stepped into the cold.

Now in the light of day, Gene sadly shook his head. God, how he did loath what he was being called upon to do. He had grown up with horses, always had been fond of them and remembered being in the barn this time of the morning, relishing the sounds the horses made; the lifting of feet, the stamping, the clicking of iron shoes. They coughed, snorted, nuzzled, bit, squealed and shuffled. He could smell the barn even now; the stench of hot urine spiking through scents of hay, grain, sweat, manure.

Gene looked to his partner. The kid's eyes were wide in excitement and anticipation. His sleeves were rolled above his elbows and the light brown hair on his white forearms reflected the softness of the emerging day. Quiet stretched like a strand of fine wire.

The bay mare was the first to have the wildness in her soul raise an alarm. Something in the world was slightly askew. She pricked her ears. A magpie standing on her withers felt her muscles tense and walked the length of her spine.

The stud noticed the movement of the bird and the nervousness of his mare. He arched his neck, raised his tail and took a few tentative steps forward. A weak dust devil swirled enough air to tease the stallion's smoky mane and sunlight broke apart and reflected off individual strands. To the east a flock of red-winged blackbirds began making a shrill racket. The high-strung stallion trotted back and forth and all the while his eyes were searching the horizon. The tips of ears flicked and he snorted through wide, quivering nostrils.

The stud sensed the vibrations that came from a spinning propeller even before the pinprick of noise signaled the arrival of the airplane. He reared, pawed the earth, squealed and drove his band away. Behind them the noise of the gasoline engine spilled over the open country, pushing outward from the source with the power of a tsunami.

"Oh boy!" exclaimed the kid. "Here we go."

Here we go indeed, thought Gene. He readied himself, flexing his right fist, forefinger touching the seam of his leather work glove. He filled the magazine of his rifle with cold shells and levered a live round into the chamber. Metal slapped metal.

The pilot advanced and began driving the small herd by making lazy figure-eights behind them. The horses moved on a straight course, dust rising behind them. The shooters hunkered behind boulders. The kid cackled, "Son of a gun is going to put them right in our laps."

Gene's mouth had gone dry. He exhaled and did not, or could not, inhale. The air that remained in his lungs quickly grew stale. The rifle butt was against his right shoulder and as dutifully as a soldier, under direct orders from a commanding officer, he squinted and lined up the buckhorn sites at the chest of the bay with four white stockings. In that instant he did not pause to contemplate the consequences of his action, merely waited and when she was within range he dispassionately squeezed the trigger. The tip of the barrel recoiled and rose. The thick muscles of Gene's shoulder absorbed the kick of the stock.

Out in front the mare quit running. Her legs buckled and she rolled and tumbled on the ground in what seemed to be a rapid, distinct and emphatic series of grainy black and white snapshots. So many conflicting and competing sights and sounds came at Gene that no single thing was distinguishable until he became aware of three quick shots being fired. Boom. Boom. Boom.

The kid had reloaded but failed to hit the only wild horse remaining alive, the black colt that galloped into a slight depression on his spindly legs and disappeared from sight.

"Dammit," howled the kid. "It got away. But hey, I got the stallion and two more! How many did you shoot? Just that one?"

Gene was transfixed, imagining the panic and pain that must have sizzled through the mare at the instant the hot metal slammed into her ribs and tore a hole through her pulsing heart. He wanted to cry, to run away, but had the strength for neither. He was lost in the profound and cruel bluntness of his actions and was swept away by guilt. As he lowered the rifle he became aware of a magpie in the distance that squawked and would not shut up. When he looked toward the noise he saw the lifeless mound of reddish brown hide a hundred yards away. The mare's eyes were beginning to glaze over with a bluish haze, red blood was turning the gray soil a dark crimson. Soon the sun would warm the corpse and it would begin to bloat. By afternoon the scavengers would have eaten their fill, leaving the remains to the insects and the natural processes of decay.

Gene felt the weight of the rifle in his hands. He had killed this horse. For what reason? Because the Forest Service told him to do it. The policy of the federal government was to clear the range of all mustangs. Without competition from wild horses there would be more feed for deer and better grazing for cattle. To some bureaucrat in Washington, D.C., such action seemed logical, but to Gene the killing was a senseless and shameful act. It was wrong. His breathing now came in shallow, ragged gasps. His head hung low. His body swayed. He absently ran his thumb along the spine of the rifle's barrel. He stood rooted to one spot, alone in his personal misery, and then slowly, as if it were a contest and gravity was winning, his knees bent and he slumped to the ground.

The kid was down on the flat standing over the stallion. He withdrew his knife, cut off a hunk of the smoke-colored mane and waved it like a triumphant cavalry soldier flourishing an enemy scalp. "Hey Gene, get the camera. Take my picture."

Ray rode in from checking the cows and calves. He put his horse away and went to the milk stall. Herman had his head leaned into the holstein and a steady cadence was sending squirts of frothy milk into the tin bucket. The cow swished her tail in his face.

"Stop that," Herman reprimanded her. He threw over his shoulder to Ray, "Heard you shoot. Get another coyote?"

"Naw," said Ray. The streams of milk counted time. "Real nice brown mare was walking the fence line. Lower jaw was blown off. I put her out of her misery."

The drumming of the milk ceased. Herman turned on the stool. "Shot?"

"Yep," said Ray.

"Who would do that?"

"Don't know," said Ray.

"Probably the same kind who would line up Indian skulls and use them for target practice," said Herman, and with a sad shake of his head he returned to milking.

A colt, black as coal without a single marking, wandered into the ranch headquarters at Steele Swamp. He was leggy and pretty and was starving. Betty fixed him a bottle of milk and Herman and Ray held the little fellow while she coaxed him into nursing from the nipple.

They babied the colt and came to calling him Little Black Beauty. Within a few days Little Black Beauty not only became domesticated but was making a pest of himself. He took up residence near the back door and whenever anyone stepped outside he charged that person, butting with his head, demanding to be fed. For the first few days it was fun but soon Little Black Beauty became absolutely spoiled and a nuisance. Herman took him to a stall in the barn where they continued to bottle feed him.

The Vowells had finished supper and Herman and Ray were headed outside to do chores when a Forest Service pickup drove into ranch headquarters. It came to an unsteady stop, rolled a few feet and the engine coughed, sputtered and died. The passenger was a young man. He remained seated. The driver got out, patted the fender, moved forward. Herman recognized him immediately. They had buckarooed together.

Herman walked in his direction. "Hello, Gene." They shook hands. "What brings you this way?"

Gene had taken off his Stetson and was nervously fingering the crease of the crown. He cleared his throat. "Herman, orders got sent down from headquarters, said we were supposed to clean the range of wild horses. I said it was a mistake. Said there's some fine horses running loose. Horses most anyone be proud to own. Didn't make no difference to the higher ups.

"Herman, I hated like hell to be a part of a thing like this, but I can't afford to lose my job and have to go back to buckarooing. That's a young man's game. I'm too damn old." He replaced his hat. "I just thought you ought to know what's been going on, Herman." He waited for some reaction from Herman. If Herman were to punch him in the mouth he would stand and take it. Gene had it coming and knew it. But it unnerved him when Herman did nothing, said nothing, just stood there staring off into the distance.

When Herman finally did speak he gritted his teeth and it seemed as though he was having to force the air over his vocal cords. "How many? How many did you kill, Gene?"

"Up north, along state line, 77 head. The kid there in the rig, he was on the flat and wounded a stud. It turned on him, was coming hard and the kid ran out of shells. He tried to reload, panicked, fumbled his shells and I had half a mind to let nature take its course. But in the end I couldn't. I shot the stud ten paces from where the kid stood. Shook him up pretty bad. Hasn't been the same since. Shocky I guess. Serves him right. Shooting wild horses ain't a sport.

"Down in Pothole Valley we killed 400, maybe 450. Pretty much wiped the country clean."

"Those were the best horses of all." Herman was close to tears. "My favorites have all come from Pothole. How could you do something like that, Gene?"

"Orders are orders. I feel plumb bad about it. I never had a

choice. I had to. Dammit Herman, I'm sorry." Gene slammed a
fist into his open hand and returned to the government pickup.
In his haste to get away he spun the tires and ground gears
shifting to third.

Ray stepped forward. He stared at the trail of dust and said,
"God help us."

There had always been an intense pleasure in being
horseback, looking out over a flat and watching the blaze of a
sunrise push crimson and golden highlights across the soft curves
of the land. And if a man allowed his gaze to follow the natural
drainage, to a swale where the tall grasses waved with the
movement of the wind, a few head of wild horses would likely be
found there, standing together as a family, lazily swishing their
tails, quietly celebrating the coming of a new day.

The elimination of the wild horses from the Devil's Garden
took away that joy. Herman and Betty talked about what it meant
to them. They felt they had been robbed of the one thing they
held dearest to their hearts. Betty, with tears stinging her eyes,
said it best. "I remember when you first brought me here,
Herman. You pointed out that black stallion and his band of
mares and you told me they were wild horses. I was utterly
thrilled. The wild horses represented so much to me. They were
a link to the past, to the Old West. They were untamed. They
were free and wild. And now they're gone and nothing seems
right any more."

FOURTEEN

As one era ended, another began. The mechanical revolution intruded on Steele Swamp in the form of a washing machine. Mr. Dalton brought it to the ranch and told Betty, "It will save time."

But the washing machine was a stubborn contraption. It was powered by a gasoline engine and outfitted with a foot lever that had to be kicked downward to turn over the motor. On wash day Herman worked himself into a lather trying to get the engine to run. Herman loathed anything mechanical, especially if it involved what he referred to as an "infernal combustion engine". He wore a hole in the sole of one boot kicking the lever. And when the motor finally did catch it belched white smoke and spewed stinky fumes that always gave Betty a headache before the day was over. But in her mind it was better than the alternatives, a scrub board or the long-handled plunger designed to suck dirt out of clothes.

The next mechanical device to arrive at Steele Swamp was a kerosene-powered Servel refrigerator. It replaced the cool box, a screened compartment where a copper boiler dripped water over gunnysacks. The Servel had a freezer compartment and it was a luxury to have ice cream in the heat of summer without having to hand-crank the old ice cream maker every time.

On one of his trips to the ranch Mr. Dalton announced to Betty she had cleaned her last glass chimney and that she could throw away her Coleman lamps and Aladdin lanterns. He had brought her a light plant and from that day forward he promised electricity would light their way. He had an electrician with him to set it up and wire the house. The light plant did work but the engine could be temperamental and sometimes stop running for want of a small part or for no apparent reason at all. Betty kept her lamps and lanterns handy and used them in emergencies. And, of course, she kept her wood stove. The light plant was not designed to carry the load necessary to operate an electric stove, and besides, Betty and the men thought food tasted best when cooked on a wood stove.

Herman surprised Betty with a Motorola radio. In the evenings Herman and Betty, Ray when he was there, and sometimes a hired man or two, gathered in the kitchen and listened to "The Shadow" or "Fibber Magee and Mollie".

Before haying season Mr. Dalton purchased a fleet of International Harvester equipment; tractors, mowing machines and mechanical balers. He explained to Herman. "The reason I made the change now is because it's getting harder and harder to find teamsters. Since the war the whole world has changed. Everything has speeded up. If we're going to stay with the times we have to go mechanical. It's simply a matter of efficiency."

Always before the meadow had been relatively quiet. There would be the occasional whinny, the voices of men talking, the clank of a rake or the soft swish of the mower blades sliding back and forth. But now, as Betty worked in the garden, the meadow resounded to the snap and pop of gasoline motors and the loud "chunk-chunk-chunk" of the balers.

One night, as they lay in bed, Herman told Betty, "A big change has come to our little corner of the world. And it hasn't been for the better."

When the baled hay had been collected and piled in square stacks Mr. Dalton paid a visit to the ranch. He instructed Herman, "I want you to round up the work horses and drive them to Dry Lake. I've arranged for trucks to haul them off to the chicken feed plant. We don't have any more use for work horses. Doesn't make sense to carry them through another winter."

Herman and Ray drove the work horses to Dry Lake and stood watching as they were loaded in stock trucks and taken away. As they rode home memories of particular horses and the men who drove them played on their minds.

"Know what I'm going to miss most?" asked Herman and he did not wait for a reply from Ray. "The clatter of those old mowing machines. I'm even going to miss the runaways. We had some good teamsters and we had some dandies who couldn't have driven a team of mice to a cheese factory. Remember Winnemucca? Cranky old coot. You're the one that gave him the name as I recall."

"That's where he said he came from," stated Ray.

Herman remembered Winnemucca's round, red face; the shoes he had cut to ribbons because of his numerous corns and bunions; his baggy pants held up by a piece of twine he crossed from one shoulder to the other. "I'm thinking of the time Winnemucca was leading Ike and Strip from the barn and a horse broke away and came past. Scared Ike and Strip and they took off in opposite directions. Winnemucca tried to hold on and when those horses came to the ends of their halter ropes they lifted that poor little man completely off the ground and that was when his twine suspenders broke and his pants fell down around his ankles. I can still hear the men laughing. Remember that?"

"I wasn't there," said Ray. "But you told me about it."

"Abe, now that fellow was a classic. I put him on a mower

with the gentlest team. I checked on him and he was sitting on the ground in front of his mower blade casually swatting flies and munching on a stem of grass between his teeth. I kept my voice steady and calm, told him that by golly, he was going to kill himself and to get the heck away from in front of that blade. The mower was in gear and if those horses moved that sickle was sure as heck going to cut him in two. I don't think I ever convinced Abe of the danger he was facing but he finally did move. The next day his team spooked and ran away. He fell off the back of the mower and was lucky he didn't get hurt. I roped the team, brought them back, even let Abe finish out the day and when he came in that evening I gave him his pay and drove him to town. Figured he was nothing more than a serious accident looking for a place to happen."

"Yeah, you had your problems," said Ray.

Herman went on, "Remember the time Darky stepped on Smitty's toe? And remember Bill, now there was a notorious runaway horse. I don't believe we ever got through a haying without him tearing up a mower or a rake. And Jack? He ran in the hills as a stud until he was six and we never got around to breaking him until he was eight. Put those two together and they were a snuffy team to handle but a good team for a good man."

"Herman," said Ray. "I remember every one of those horses. So why don't you just be quiet for a while and let me remember them on my own."

Without a work horse on the place, Herman and Ray had to use a tractor to pull the hay sled that winter. And since the tractor could not be trained like the horses to make a big slow circle on its own, a weight was attached to a wire and hung on the steering wheel. It worked most of the time, except when the front wheel hit the rise of a check dam and then the tractor would veer off course and Herman or Ray would have to jump down and reset the wheel and the weight.

In February an Arctic front moved in and the temperature dropped to forty below zero. The tractor was parked in the blacksmith shop and every morning a fire had to be built. While the tractor was warming the hungry cows would stand near the gate and bellow and bawl to show their displeasure at the delay.

The biggest change of all that came to Steele Swamp had nothing to do with mechanics and machinery. It had everything to do with emotions, needs, yearnings and desires. At the age of 36 Betty wanted a baby. She realized that if she were to conceive again the likelihood of her having another tubal pregnancy was too great to accept the risks. But she wanted a baby; a baby to hold in her arms, a baby to nurture and love. A baby to raise.

Betty made up her mind that the only practical alternative to her becoming pregnant was to adopt. But when she broached the subject with Herman he stated his firm opinion. "No. No way. Absolutely not."

"But why?"

"I don't want some hand-me-down kid."

"But think of it, Herman, a little baby of our own." Betty held her arms cradled to her chest. Empty arms.

"We have each other," said Herman. "That's plenty enough."

Betty cried. And in the days and weeks ahead it seemed that she cried at the drop of a hat. Most often tears came when she was alone in the kitchen, other times she would be helping Herman work cattle and see a frisky calf playing or a heartbroken mother bellowing for a calf that had been stillborn or momentarily lost. Tears would come. Betty was powerless to stop them. Always the tears were there, lurking just below the surface, waiting for any trivial excuse to boil over and spill down her cheeks.

Herman witnessed Betty's anguish and over time he felt his refusal to consider adoption begin to waver ever so slightly. In the end it came down to a promise made. Both times he had nearly lost Betty he had promised God that if He would spare her life, Herman would make sure he did whatever he could to make Betty happy. Having a baby would bring her happiness and be the culmination of her womanly dreams and ambitions.

One evening, when they were alone, Herman shocked Betty by telling her, "I know you want a baby. I want you to be happy. I'm not one hundred percent for this thing but if you want to look into adoption I don't have a problem with seeing what's out there."

Betty threw her arms around him. "Oh Herman, I love you so much."

On July 31, 1956 a young woman in Medford, Oregon gave birth to a healthy girl. The following day Betty received a phone call from the young woman's attorney. He asked if Betty wanted the baby. She told him yes, most definitely yes.

Haying season was in full swing and Herman was at the edge of the field working on a piece of equipment when he looked up and saw Betty running toward him, apron flapping. When she reached him she was winded but managed to say, "We have a baby."

"We what?"

"Have a baby. We have a baby."

"When did this come about?"

She took several deep breaths. "I've been talking with an attorney. He just called. He has a baby girl for us. In Medford. Oh, Herman, aren't you thrilled? Aren't you ready to burst? I want to leave right now. Can we, darling?"

"Not so fast. I thought you were just checking into things. I didn't know you had a baby on order." Herman tried to step back, put some distance between himself and his delirious wife.

"It just happened," said Betty, not losing any of her momentum. "God took pity on us. It's His gift. Oh, thank You, Lord. Thank You so much."

"But we're in the middle of haying. I've got a crew to look after. You've got meals to cook."

Betty acted as though she did not hear a word he said. "It's a baby girl. What do you think about Susan Lee? Isn't that a pretty name? Can we leave this minute?"

"What about the crew? Who's going to cook?"

"I'll call Mildred. I know she'll come out. Can you believe it, Herman? Our baby. Our very own baby. Susan Lee Vowell. We'll call her Susie."

Herman and Betty drove to Medford and back home in one long day and most of the night. On the return trip Betty clutched the precious bundle of joy in her arms. She loved the feeling of holding the beautiful baby and the way little Susie looked up at her with those big brown eyes.

It was not until well after midnight, when they finally turned onto the dirt road that led to the ranch, that Susie fell asleep. Betty kept turning on a flashlight and shining it on Susie's face to make sure she was breathing. She was still asleep at 3 a.m. when they arrived at Steele Swamp. Betty put Susie down in their bed, tucked her in, gave her a kiss on both precious cheeks, laid with her and took a fifteen-minute nap and then went to the kitchen and began cooking breakfast for the crew.

Ray and the buckaroo crew had happened to arrive late the evening before and when Betty gave Ray the news he immediately wanted to see Susie. Betty protested, "But she's asleep."

"I want to see her," said Ray. "She's my niece. Go get her. You don't have to wake her. Just bring her in here. One minute. A quick peek. That's all. Please."

"My goodness, Ray," said Betty, drying her hands on her apron. She was grinning. "That's more words than I've heard you string together in your entire life. Okay, I'll bring her out. But I want everyone to be quiet. Don't wake her. It was a long night.

She's tired."

Betty brought Susie to the dining room and the men oohed
and aahed. Susie did wake up. She started crying. Uncle Ray took
her from Betty. He held her in his arms and paced back and forth
in the kitchen, talking to Susie soft and gentle, the same tone and
words he used to reassure a foal, and in a little bit Susie went back
to sleep. Ray rocked her in his arms for a few minutes more and
handed her to Betty.

"I think you got yourself a keeper," he whispered.

Betty arranged a modest nursery in one of the bedrooms.
One day Herman came in to check on Susie and as he stepped
into the room he breathed in all the delicate fragrances of
powders and lotions, baby smells. It made him feel complete and
fulfilled.

Susie was awake and peeping through the crib bars at some
dancing light on the opposite wall. As he stepped closer she
heard the familiar tromp of his boots and turned her head. A big,
gummy smile spread across her round face and her arms and legs
waved like seaweed in a tidal pool. She opened her arms,
wanting Herman to pick her up, and he did. He lifted her to his
shoulder and she cooed. He gently patted her back with two
fingers and said aloud, "I love you, little darling."

At that moment Herman thought he had finally come to a
true understanding of Betty's desperate longing for a child. This
baby had filled a hole in his being that he never knew existed.
Susie knit them together as a family. In his heart Herman knew
his life had never been so worthwhile. He said a silent prayer in
gratitude.

Thanksgiving and Christmas were spent snowbound at the
ranch. Ray was there and he was just as proud of Susie as her
parents. He fed her formula, burped her, read to her and rocked
her to sleep. Sometimes Betty and Herman almost had to fight
him to get their turn. It was a standing joke that Susie would grow

up thinking that Ray was both her mother and father. But when spring rolled around Ray went back to buckarooing and it was two months before he drifted back to Steele Swamp. When he did he was amazed at how much "my little girl" had grown.

Susie walked at sixteen months and was outdoors as often as she was inside. Betty would set her in front of her on the saddle and Susie clutched the saddle horn, giggled and made cooing sounds like a mourning dove as she bounced along.

By the time Susie was 20 months old she was helping Herman bring in firewood. She would carry small pieces from the stack to the wheelbarrow. Herman praised her. And when the wheelbarrow was full he hefted her to the top of the load and wheeled her to the house. At milking time Susie accompanied Herman to the barn and patiently waited while her daddy filled the bucket and then tried to help carry it to the milk room. She was with Herman when he fed the horses and surely would have gone to the fields when he fed the cows if Betty had allowed it. Even before Susie turned two years old Herman had her riding horseback, by herself, while he led the gentlest horse on the ranch in circles around the corral. Susie used some of her first words to encourage him, "More, Daddy."

Mr. Dalton died of a heart attack on May 2, 1958. It was exactly 22 years since Herman went to work for him and 21 years since Ray came on board. Mr. Dalton's estate was divided between his two children. Billy took the farm ground and Betty Lou and her husband, Bob Byrne, took the cattle, the range land and Steele Swamp.

One evening Herman told Betty, "Nothing is the same as when Mr. Dalton was alive."

"I know," said Betty. "We can't ever go back although I think we would like to."

"I've got something to talk over with you. Ray and I have been thinking about maybe pooling our money and buying a ranch. What do you think about that?" Herman had a pretty fair idea of what she would say. It was not the first time they had discussed leaving Steele Swamp and getting a place of their own.

"I know it would be difficult leaving here," said Betty. She took her time, choosing her words carefully. "But in a few more years Susie will start school and we will need to do something. I can't imagine getting a house in town and having to live apart from you. I think we should look. If and when we find something, we can move. As for Ray, I think he would be a terrific partner. You know I love him like a brother, he's great with Susie and the two of you have always made a terrific team."

The spring of 1960 the Vowells purchased a small ranch in Langell Valley, thirty miles northwest of Steele Swamp. As the date to move drew near, Herman could feel tension building inside him. One evening after chores, he took a hike on the ridge behind the headquarters. He sat on a boulder looking out over the house, the barn and the emerald meadow beyond.

He saw memories, vivid and alive, like scenes from a favorite movie. Wild horses in winter blowing vapor from flared nostrils; a calf struggling to gain its feet and come free of the tangle of afterbirth; heading a steer and watching it swing in a slow motion arc as Ray's loop snaked around the steer's dancing hind feet. He recalled the time he came upon Betty at the swimming hole as she was getting out of the water. Above her a cloud of insects whined and night hawks swooped low, gorging themselves. A deep-throated bull frog bellowed. A fish broke the surface and ripples marched across the pond. When Betty sensed someone watching her she turned and her face caught and held the light. Her skin was damp, rose colored, softly luminous, appealing. She was smiling at him with a combination of surprise and joy, but most of all love.

Off to the west the sun was setting. Herman could feel the change through the porous rock and could sense the coolness slowly climb the column of his spine. Tomorrow, when the sun rose, nothing would be the same. A mosquito landed on Herman's forearm and he watched it with detached interest as the wonky legs set themselves against his skin. He allowed her to bite him. The tiny stab of pain made this moment real. He flexed the muscles in his forearm and they gripped and held the insect's proboscis. Unable to release she swelled with blood and finally exploded in a tiny burst of crimson. Herman licked his thumb and wiped at the blood, drying the thumb on his pant leg.

The sun was down. Shadows consumed the land. Herman rose and started off the hill knowing, as long as he lived, he would never forget Steele Swamp and the Devil's Garden.

Betty was so consumed with the work involved in boxing up a household and the complexities of the move that she did not allow herself the indulgence of a single sentimental moment. It finally hit her when everything in the house had been carried out by friends and loaded into a convoy of pickups, horse trailers and stock trucks. She went inside to see if there was anything they might have missed. On one empty wall was an outline where the photograph of wild horses had hung for so many years. The corner of the living room, freshly swept, was where the decorated tree sat every Christmas. Here in the kitchen was where Susie's high chair had been....

"Mommy, Mommy. Come on, Mommy," Susie was calling.

Betty pulled the door shut behind her.

The Vowells quickly settled in and began breaking and working horses on their ranch in Langell Valley. Their years of experience served them well and when word made the rounds that the Vowell brothers were in the business of training horses, the phone started ringing and it did not stop. The Vowells had colts to break, problem horses that needed cured of bad habits and cutting horses that required fine tuning.

Each horse brought to the Vowell ranch was given individual attention. Herman and Ray operated on the philosophy that if a horse was afraid it would not and could not learn. They never used rough methods but methodically moved through each step – halter breaking, getting the animal used to the human touch, handling its feet, accepting a bridle, a bit, a saddle blanket, a saddle and finally the weight of a rider.

Wild horses were the easiest to break because they had no bad habits to overcome and they paid attention to a man. The toughest horses to work with were those that had been spoiled by someone who did not know what he or she was doing, or who had tried to use bullying and intimidation. Those animals had to unlearn everything they knew before a level of trust could be established and the process of re-training begin.

The Vowell brothers built a solid reputation for breaking and training horses. Nearly every day someone asked Herman or Ray to work a particular horse. It reached the point of success where they had to limit the number of horses on the ranch or there would not be enough hours in the day to work them all.

During this time Betty taught Susie to barrel race and at a very young age, even before she started first grade at Bonanza Elementary School, Susie was competing and winning local competitions.

Everything seemed to have fallen into place for the Vowells. Herman and Ray had a ranch of their own. They were working together, making a good living doing what they loved. Betty was happy and little Susie was growing up and becoming a terrific hand and a skilled rider. Life could not have been better.

FIFTEEN

Betty lived with a dark secret. Shortly after they moved from Steele Swamp to the Langell Valley ranch she noticed a small lump on the outside of her left breast. She hoped it would go away on its own but over time the lump grew in both size and density. She ignored it. Finally the swelling began to bother her to the point it was difficult to raise her left arm. The day came when she felt compelled to share her secret with Herman.

In a very matter-of-fact tone she stated, "I suppose I ought to see a doctor."

Betty was never sick. Herman asked, "Whatever for?"

She took his hand, held it to the side of her left breast. "Feel this."

He was alarmed that the lump was so large, so solid, that it had such mass to it. He was shocked he had not known it was there. "How long have you had this?"

"A while," she said. "I don't think it's anything to be overly concerned about but I suppose I should have it looked at."

"Call Dr. Tice. Make an appointment, today if you can. I'll drive you," said Herman.

As Betty went to the house to make the call Herman watched her walk away. It seemed that her clothes were hanging on her. Why had he not noticed she was losing weight? He was scared and tried to concentrate on his breathing while a physical pain gripped him like talons. He tried to struggle against this pain but it simply tightened its grip. He staggered around the corner of the barn and dropped down on a bale of hay. He breathed through his mouth, never tasting the sweetness of the freshly mowed alfalfa or the freshness of the air on his tongue, only the sharply metallic tang of fear. He concentrated on breathing in and breathing out.

Betty stepped onto the back porch and even though Herman was out of sight she knew he was nearby and called to him, said she had scheduled an appointment for 3 o'clock that afternoon. He swallowed hard, managed to call back to her, "Okay, Sugar. Better plan on leaving no later than two."

After that he stood. He dug in his hind pocket and removed his wallet, withdrew a photograph of Betty taken the year they were married. It was frayed at the edges. He stared at her likeness for the longest time, then put it away and stepped inside the barn.

Coming in from the burnished sunlight the barn was a refuge of murky gray and somber shadows. A horse nickered and Herman stepped to his stall but was unable to distinguish anything but the horse's outline. The heat of the day dissipated. The temperature dropped a full ten degrees. The horse came to nuzzle him but Herman turned away from the affection and listened to his own hollow footfalls as he walked to where the oats were kept. He filled a coffee can, returned to the stall and poured the contents into the trough for the horse. For a time he stood in the strange pallor of light, listening to the horse chew, a blunted, rhythmic, raspy sound. He thought ahead to the upcoming trip to town, the trip to the doctor's office. Betty would slide over next to him on the seat like they were teenage lovers going out on a date. The radio would be dialed to the country western station that originated in Alturas. They would listen to Hank Williams sing with that dry, lonely, nasal twang of his. If they came home as the sun was going down, the last song of the day would be "Red Sails in the Sunset" and then the station would go off the air. They would ride the last few miles in silence. By that time Dr. Tice would have examined Betty. They would have a pretty good idea of what was wrong. Neither of them would want to talk. And now Herman prayed that the lump in her breast would not be as serious as he feared. But in the back of his mind he already knew that it was all that bad and more.

When they lived at Steele Swamp Herman always hired old broken down buckaroos to help out around the place. They stayed a month, a year or several years. Tuc, Charlie, Sam, Fred.... They ate in the house, were given a cot in the bunkhouse and a little pay on the side, not because they could contribute like a young buckaroo but because Herman had a respect for their years of steady service as well as their stubborn deterioration. He accepted their smoking and the accompanying coughing fits that went on until they hawked up a mouthful of old-man phlegm. As soon as the coughing jag ended they went right back to rolling another cigarette, lighting it and inhaling smoke in well-practiced and satisfying drags. They drank whiskey whenever they had it, their Adam's apple bobbing up and down like an extra elbow, and a few moments later the whiskey would work its magic and mask their pain and they could move again, shuffling around. At times they grimaced, grunted and groaned. Their skin turned white as milled flour but places on their face and on the back of their hands were blotched, as though rusted through. Their cheeks were sunken. Teeth were missing. They squinted to bring the world into focus. Day by day these men wasted away with unseen diseases or simply old age consuming them. Herman wondered if this was the way it would be with Betty. Would the disease eat away at her until nothing remained?

Dr. Tice delivered the worst news possible. Betty had breast cancer. Betty knew what a cancer death was like. She and Lee had been with their mother when Leona died of pancreatic cancer in 1956. It had been a terrible time.

"The breast will have to be removed as soon as possible," said Dr. Tice. He referred to the procedure as a "radical mastectomy".

Betty calmly accepted the diagnosis. Way back when she had first felt the lump, and all those months when the area itched and the tumor grew, she knew it was cancer. And now, sitting on the edge of the examining table, arms wrapped around herself, she was reconciled to giving up the infected breast in order to spare her life.

She thought back twenty-some years, to when her breasts first appeared like pink apple blossoms on her chest. They had graced her life with feminine beauty. She was thankful for the years she had possessed them. She had to be strong and backhanded a single tear that slid down her cheek.

Dr. Tice was still talking. He was saying words that seemed to be camouflaged because Betty was not able to unravel their meaning. He mentioned, "tumor, metastasis, recurrence, progression of disease", and concluded that if the cancer had reached her lymph nodes, as he feared it had, the disease was "inevitably fatal".

Betty folded her hands tightly together, as if in prayer. Her eyes were dry. She said to Dr. Tice, "This can't be happening. Not to me. I have a daughter to raise."

Dr. Tice said, "I know this is difficult to accept...."

Betty reacted angrily. "No, you're not hearing me. I have a daughter to raise. I can't die."

Dr. Tice lowered his voice. "I'm sorry." He bit his lip to keep his emotions from showing.

"How long do I have?"

"Hard to say. We will take the breast and put you on a program of radiation treatments. I don't know how long." He paused. "Maybe five years, if you're lucky."

"And if I'm not lucky?"

"A year, two years."

"Then I'll use my luck and take five years," said Betty and the anger was gone and she was struggling to smile. The smile quickly dissipated. "This will kill poor Herman. What do I tell him?"

"Tell him the truth," was Dr. Tice's advice. He walked to the door and turned. "He will simply have to learn to handle it." He stepped outside, pulled the door closed and stood there. It took him a moment before he could go on. He remembered the first time he saw Betty, lying on the makeshift operating table in the kitchen at the ranch. She had survived that operation because she was a fighter. She had so much to live for then and even more now. He knew Betty was right, this was going to kill Herman.

Betty sat on the examination table and said a prayer for Herman, that his soul would find comfort. She prayed for Susie, that she would understand and forgive her mother for having to leave this earth before her work was finished. She prayed for Ray. And then she broke down and cried, sobbing uncontrollably into her splayed fingers. Her breath came as loud as the wind blowing through the juniper boughs on the ridge above Steele Swamp and her thoughts drifted to those pleasant times when the snow drifted the road closed and isolated them from the outside world. She recalled the overwhelming comfort she had felt in knowing the pantry shelves were filled with canned vegetables from the garden. Potatoes, carrots and onions were in a sawdust pit. Hams and sides of bacon had been smoked and cured. The chickens had grain. The milk cow had plenty of hay. The supplies were all stacked in their proper place. In the evening the coyotes came close to the house and provided company with their serenades. And during the days the hawks and eagles circled, flashing in the light-struck sky and Betty would have to shield her eyes as she watched them spiral wider and higher. Back then she had been completely happy, satisfied and content with her perfect life.

Before the surgery Betty tried to prepare Susie. "Sweetie, Mommy is going to go to the hospital for a few days."

"What's wrong, Mommy?"

"I have a lump right here," said Betty pointing to a spot near her left breast. "The doctors are going to make it go away."

"And then you will be all better?"

"Yes," smiled Betty. "And then Mommy will be all better."

Still dressed in his surgical suit, Dr. Tice came to the waiting room, where Herman sat with Ray and Betty's sister Lee. He drew Herman away from the others and told him, "The tumor was big and very aggressive. It had spread. We did a single mastectomy and removed fourteen lymph nodes."

Herman shook his head. He crossed his arms over his chest. He tried to keep his voice steady. "Did you get it all?"

"Herman, there was no way we could get it all. She waited too long. She didn't give us any options. She will recover from the operation but I can almost guarantee there will be a recurrence of the cancer. And when it does return.... I'm sorry, Herman." Dr. Tice patted Herman's shoulder and stepped around him.

The hospital room was flooded with flowers and cards. Betty was too sick to enjoy them. The day after her mastectomy she complained of a strange sensation in her chest and underarm. It was not exactly numb, she said, but more of a non-feeling. And she said there was an overall tightness in her rib cage. The nurse who came to help with physical therapy said those were all normal, post-operative sensations. She helped Betty lift her left arm. She said it was important to keep the arm mobile, that scar tissue was much harder to stretch if it were allowed to heal without exercise. After five days Betty was sent home.

At home, what bothered Betty most was that every time she passed a mirror she glanced at her reflection and saw the uneven symmetry of her chest. The dressing had to be changed daily and when it was removed she looked down at where the sharp scalpel had sliced off her breast. The sight of the incision filled her with a curious sense of dread that was partly revulsion and partly a casual acceptance of her perilous condition. Since she could not raise her left arm Herman helped change the dressing and wrap the flatness of her lopsided chest in the confines of an Ace bandage.

Betty worked hard to retrain her muscles. She stood near a wall, lifted the damaged arm up with her good arm, and used her fingers to crawl up the wall. Every day she made a concerted effort to walk the fingers a little higher. She washed dishes and found that by stepping on a stool she could stretch and put away the dishes in the cupboards. When she was in the shower she reached as high as possible and marked a soap line on the tiles to mark her progress.

After six weeks of diligent effort Betty could raise the arm above her head and she proudly displayed her accomplishment to her family. Herman applauded enthusiastically. Susie did not display any emotion. Herman chided her, saying, "Susie, aren't you going to clap for Mommy?"

"I don't want to," said Susie.

"That's okay," said Betty. She went to Susie and wrapped her arms around her in a tight embrace. "Mommy loves you."

"I know," said Susie.

The same radiation used to create an X-ray was used in high-energy doses and localized to a specific area to destroy cancer cells. But the very notion of radiation treatment as a cure bothered Betty more than the disease. She reasoned that if the radiation killed bad cells and that was good, it must also kill good cells and that was bad. She remembered that when the atom bombs were dropped on Japan many more people died from radiation than from the actual bomb blast. Radiation killed people. But Dr. Tice said, in Betty's case, radiation was absolutely essential. He promised it would buy her additional time to be a wife and mother. Even though Betty feared the radiation she clung to the hope it might prolong her life.

At the beginning of the therapy the radiologist laid Betty on a horizontal apparatus that molded to her body. The body mold was to assure the exact position during each of the upcoming treatments. When she was securely in place, with her left arm painfully extended over her head, a huge cobalt radiation machine was aimed at a spot just below, and to the left, of where her breast had been.

"Don't move anything. Just breathe," the radiologist instructed. He left the room, closed the door and stepped behind a protective lead shield. A red light came on. The monster machine whined and clicked as its shutters opened. Betty closed her eyes. She could feel the X-rays invade her body. Time passed with agonizing slowness. Every few seconds, zap-zap-zap, and then a pause and again, zap-zap-zap.

An amplified voice boomed, "Not much longer. Don't move."

The red light went off. There was a sharp click and the machine stopped making noises. Betty thought the treatment was over and began to relax but the radiologist opened the door, changed the field and went back out, closing the door, starting the machine once again. Zap-zap-zap.

The next time Herman took Betty to the radiation center for her treatment the radiologist could not find her chart. He had no record of her ever having been there.

"Look at my face," said Betty. "Do I look familiar to you?"

The radiologist was a tall, gangly fellow, not much more than thirty years old. He had adopted a retarded personality as a defense against putting a face on his patients. He did not want to know them as human beings. Most were going to die anyway. He wanted, needed, distance from them.

"I treat a lot of patients," he explained to Betty.

Her chin shuddered in response to his heartless remark. She knew that in a different situation, a different time, with a fancy dress, a few strokes of makeup and a touch of lipstick she most certainly could have turned this man's head. He would not have forgotten her. She bit her lip as she answered him, her voice beginning to crack. "But you treat us one at a time."

Herman drove Betty to the radiation sessions twice a week, while Ray stayed with Susie. On those days friends brought food for the family. On the other days Betty continued her household chores with single-minded diligence; cooking, washing clothes, dusting, scrubbing floors, watering plants and gathering eggs from the hen house. She read to Susie. She drank milk shakes laced with eggs and protein powder. She slept more. Sometimes in the middle of the night she would get up and sit in front of the blue flicker of the TV screen. She was thirsty all the time but it was difficult for her to swallow. Her palms sweated. Her stomach churned. She experienced bouts of nausea, debilitating headaches and prolonged periods of dizziness. Her face became puffy and her skin as dry and thick as leather chaps.

It seemed to Betty that cancer was weaving its hideous thread through every minute, every hour, every day, every week of her existence. In her mind the shift from being alive to being dead became distorted and blurred. Her bones weakened. Her muscles softened. She felt her body melting like a snowman in the heat of July. Sometimes her emotions welled up inside and the only thing she could do was cry them away.

Betty wore the same clothes and coat to each treatment. When she completed the six-week program she came home, stripped off the coat and clothes, took a shower, put on fresh clothes and some makeup.

"I can't stand them. They stink," she told Herman, motioning to the pile of clothes.

"We can fix that," said Herman. He scooped up the offending garments and marched to the burn barrel. After liberally dousing them with diesel he lit them on fire. When he returned to the house Betty wrapped her arms around his waist and told him, "Thank you."

"Sweetheart, it tore me up inside seeing you having to go through all that," Herman told her.

"I know it did," she said.

"It's over with now."

"Thank goodness. If I had one more treatment I'm sure it would kill me."

Weeks passed and Betty was getting back on her feet. One warm day she drifted down to watch Herman and Ray work the horses. She marveled at their ability to teach a green colt to become a trustworthy saddle horse.

She wandered to another corral where wild horses paced nervously. They reminded her of the mustangs of Devil's Garden but she recalled Herman mentioning that a truckload of wild horses had been captured on Tableland, a vast country north of Sprague River, and brought to the ranch to be broken.

Betty stepped closer. Domestic horses smelled of saddle blankets and leather. These mustangs did not smell like that. Their sweat had not been sweetened by alfalfa hay and processed grain. Their hooves were not stained with the rankness that came from standing in their own manure. They had never been touched by a brush or curry comb. Their hair was long and shaggy, their tails and manes were matted with sticktights and foxtails. These Tableland mustangs smelled of sage and mountain mahogany, of freshwater springs that bubbled out of the ground, of wide open spaces, sunny skies and star-studded nights. The herd moved as one, like a school of fish driven into shallow water, roiling in and out and around and through one another. The colors mixing, eyes rolling, ears flicking, snorting, rearing, biting, occasionally kicking. They were frightened. They were curious. Betty reveled in their wildness.

She returned to the house to fix dinner and when Herman came in she asked him if he would saddle her horse, Pokey.

"Are you sure you're ready?"

She was not sure of anything and did not answer right away. Instead she opened the screen door, walked outside to the porch and sat on the railing. Herman followed. She was thinking about the wild horses. She flashed him a confident smile. "I'm ready," she said.

He placed a calloused hand lightly on her shoulder and gently told her, "You've been pushing yourself pretty hard. I don't want you to overdo it."

Betty wanted to shout at him that she needed to get on with life; that she wanted to forget she had ever had cancer. Since she was fitted with the padding to replace her missing breast she had been feeling more like a woman again. A healthy woman. More feminine. Alive.

"Herman, I want to ride. I must."

"Okay," was all Herman said.

That afternoon, with a little help from Herman, Betty was able to hoist herself onto Pokey's back. She rode circles in the round corral, never going beyond an easy lope. Being back in the saddle, with a good horse under her, buoyed Betty's spirits. She was confident that everything would work out and that God would answer her prayers and grant her the time necessary to raise Susie.

SIXTEEN

All the hard work, the minor successes and major triumphs were for naught. The cancer returned. In Betty's right breast. A simple mastectomy was performed and Betty endured more sessions of radiation treatment. This time she seemed to suffer fewer side effects. Her recovery was much quicker. Within a few months she was riding again and seemed to be enjoying life without giving any thought to Dr. Tice's dire predictions. She was going to beat this thing. She was going to be a survivor. She was going to be alive when the scientists came up with a cure for cancer.

From April through September the ranch in Langell Valley was lousy with mosquitoes. Whenever Herman and Ray went to the pasture to irrigate they were forced to wear a net over their heads so the bugs would not fly in their eyes and ears and noses and mouths. When they rode, the horses were so bothered by mosquitoes they did not have their minds on learning. And Susie could not go outside to play without a liberal dose of repellant and even then the nasty insects would bite her and she swelled up with angry welts. Besides, the Langell Valley ranch held bad memories. That was where Betty first became sick with cancer. Those memories were hard to live with.

When Herman and Ray started discussing selling the ranch and finding a new place, Betty was all for it. She asked if they could look around the town of Malin since so many of their friends lived in that area.

Once the decision to move had been made, everything quickly and conveniently fell into place. They were able to sell the Langell Valley ranch for the same price they paid for it, and they found 80 acres they could afford a few miles west of Malin. The property included a small house, a big barn and plenty of irrigated pasture. The real selling point was there were few mosquitoes.

Betty threw herself into making the new place their home. She painted the interior, put up curtains and planted flowers and a big garden. She worked so hard that Herman was afraid she might wear herself out but at the same time she was so full of life, so excited about whatever she was doing, that he bit his tongue and said nothing. Betty continued to live each moment for the moment. It was as though she thought if she kept moving the cancer would never have an opportunity to catch up to her.

If Betty was not working around the house or in the yard she was riding in the big roping arena that Herman and Ray built. She practiced barrel racing by the hour and was training a pretty little sorrel mare she called Jubilee for Susie. But each afternoon when the yellow school bus with the blinking red lights stopped on the road in front of their house Betty dropped everything she was doing and had a glass of cold milk and a plate of fresh-baked cookies waiting for Susie. They spent hours together. They had picnics. They talked and whispered and laughed. They rode horseback together. They were inseparable.

Herman and Ray continued to break horses but they also

returned to riding part-time for Bob Byrne on the Pitchfork Ranch. One morning they were headed off to brand and work cattle at Dry Lake. Betty caught up with Herman as he finished loading the saddle horses into the stock truck. "There's a jackpot barrel race in Klamath Falls today. I would kind of like to go. Would you mind hooking up the horse trailer for me?"

Herman did not respond right away. After a moment he turned toward her. He took her hands and stared at her. She was looking down. He willed her to look at him. Finally she did. Her green eyes were moist. Herman brushed at the tears on her cheeks with his fingers. He started to say something but his voice caught as he saw what her eyes were telling him.

"I can do this," she said with determination.

"I don't doubt it," said Herman. "The only thing is, you've never driven the car and pulled the horse trailer. It's kind of touchy with that much weight pushing you." He paused. "I'll hook you up. Be careful, you hear."

With that said they embraced. Betty whispered, "Thank you."

Ray came around the corner. He took one look and said, "Time we got this show on the road."

Herman and Ray spent the day at Dry Lake. They were on their way home, had just reached the highway southeast of Malin, when Herman spotted Betty barreling down the road in their white Pontiac. The horse trailer was nowhere in sight. Herman applied the brakes; they squealed from all the dust but the stock truck came to a halt. Betty stopped in her lane, effectively blocking the highway. They both rolled down their windows.

"What happened to the trailer?" shouted Herman over the roar of the truck motor.

Betty was smiling and happy. She looked like a young girl. She shouted back, "I took it off all by myself." She got out of the car then, left the door open and strolled to the truck. She climbed up on the running board and held herself there by grabbing the door with one hand and the side mirror with the other. She was only inches away from Herman. He could smell her perfume.

"So what are you doing here?" asked Herman.

"I came to tell you I won the barrel racing and it paid $35. I'm taking everyone to dinner. We're going uptown." She kissed Herman through the open window. Her hat started to fall. She grabbed it, threw back her head, laughed and jumped down. Leaning against the car, she wiggled a finger at Herman, shot him a wink, said, "Cowboy, you coming with me?"

"Sure," he said. He opened the door and crawled down.

"You drive," giggled Betty and she slid in and scooted over, but not too far.

Ray got behind the wheel and kicked the stock truck into gear. He glanced in the rear view mirror and the car was still parked, the door wide open. It appeared Herman and Betty were kissing.

Within a few months of winning the jackpot in Klamath Falls, Betty was unable to ride. The cancer had returned with a vengeance this time. She quickly became too sick, too weak, to come out of the house.

Friends quit visiting. Herman forgave them. They were brokenhearted with sorrow and seeing Betty would be like staring their own mortality in the face. They were scared and he could not blame them. He was scared, too. He knew they wanted to remember Betty as a beautiful, vivacious young woman, fun-loving and full of life. They did not want to see her reduced to skin and bones, with all the life sucked out of her by the terrible cancer.

One friend, Alice Johnson, continued to come. Several times each week she arrived at the door, always knocking softly. Herman would meet her and she would say, "I'm not interrupting anything, am I?"

Herman would tell her, "No, Alice, you're not interrupting a thing," and she would step into the hallway. Before they continued to the living room she would ask Herman if they could say a little prayer. She would take his hands and they would bow their heads together and she would speak from her heart, saying beautiful words that always inspired Herman, giving him strength and hope. And then Alice would leave him and go to Betty. Herman listened to them in the bedroom, laughing and giggling as Alice brushed Betty's hair and told her the latest gossip.

Betty ate some meals in bed but when she felt strong enough to move, she made her way to the kitchen and sat at the table while Ray cooked up a batch of sourdough hotcakes. The sourdough had been started back in 1950 from potato peelings by Herman and Ray's mother when she came to Steele Swamp to help after Betty's accident. Betty nibbled on a hotcake, or a biscuit with a little jam on it. She chewed for a long time and visited with Ray, telling him that he had turned into a pretty fair cook, and after a while, usually with a little help because she always stayed too long and overdid it, she returned to her bedroom.

The steady deterioration in Betty's health continued. One day Dr. Martin surprised them by making a house call. He examined Betty and then spoke privately with Herman. He said he could arrange to have Betty admitted to the hospital or she could die at home.

"It's come to that?" said Herman.

"Yes, it has."

Herman said he wanted to keep Betty at home. He said that was what she wanted.

"When the pain gets bad you are going to be the one who has to give her shots of morphine. You are going to have to tend to her every need. You are going to have to suffer right along with her. Can you do that, Herman?"

"Dr. Martin, it will be the hardest thing I've ever had to do in my life," said Herman. "I want to be able to do this last thing for her."

"Love is truly wondrous," said Dr. Martin. "More power to you, Herman." He extended his hand and Herman took it. And then the two men embraced. They held each other awkwardly and yet tightly. They were bound by shared emotions and their tears came swift and hard.

When the end was drawing near, Lee left her family and came up from California to stay with her sister. Lee gave Betty baths and made her look pretty with makeup, saying, "Boy oh boy, little sister, you look like you're ready to go out for a night on the town."

"I'm not going to do any such thing. But I do feel good," said Betty.

While Betty slept Lee and Herman practiced injecting a needle into an orange. The three-quarter inch needle was eased in, the plunger pulled out to check for any indication a vein had been punctured, and if there was no blood the plunger was depressed. When they were proficient at giving practice injections, and Betty was in pain, they screwed up every ounce of courage they possessed and took turns administering morphine. Each shot was recorded on a diagram of a human body so shots were never repeated in the same area.

Herman and Lee broke each day into four-hour shifts. When it was Herman's turn he sometimes lay in bed with Betty, holding her in his arms and rocking her like he used to rock baby Susie. Gently. Lovingly. At other times he sat beside her bed, holding her hand and telling her stories.

"Please pull up the shade," Betty might say. "It's too dark in here." They sat silently and watched the world through the window. An occasional car flashed past. A horse or a cow wandered into view. Once a raven landed on a fence post. Its eyes glinted black in the sunlight.

It seemed as though it had taken the two of them a lifetime to learn to sit quietly and watch the world. It was a lesson only the old or infirm seemed capable of learning. They were content being together. Silence was pure. Silence drew them closer. Betty slept. Time passed. Herman drew a breath, exhaled, drew a breath, exhaled. And he invariably noticed his breathing was in perfect unison with Betty's breathing.

One time Herman fell asleep. It was dusk when he awoke. He turned toward Betty. Her eyes were open. She was looking at him. He broke the silence, asking her, "What are you thinking about?"

She squeezed his hand, smiled, replied, "I was thinking about how much I love you."

Betty used to enjoy walking on Harpold Road in front of the house. Men on tractors waved as they passed. Drivers of hay wagons waved. In the fall the road would be littered with potatoes where they rattled free from the trucks transporting them to the cellars. If they were not damaged Betty brought them home.

Now Betty could no longer walk to the mail box, or out into the sunlight, or even to the kitchen table, or to the bathroom. She was bedridden and sodden with disease. There were times she required supplemental oxygen and clear plastic tubing ran from a machine, connected to Betty with a nasal cannula looped over her ears. But even with the oxygen her lungs were filling with fluid. She was slowly drowning. Her breathing was labored.

Herman guided a hand-held massager over her hips, her back, her shoulders. She told him it felt good. When the pain came too intensely she moaned and curled into a ball, and even if not enough time had passed since her last injection, Herman took pity and gave her another shot. She relaxed as the morphine flashed through her system. They sat together in the gloomy room. There was no direct light, only shadowy tones of gray and black. Her breathing was uneven and ragged. She stopped breathing and each time Herman wanted it to be over but then she gasped at life and the wetness in her chest rattled. She came awake crying and Herman held her until the tears stopped, tenderly brushing them from her cheeks, and again she drifted back to sleep.

Herman sat there in those tormented four-hour segments and selfishly thought, "God, when it's my turn please just take me. Don't make me suffer like this. No one deserves to suffer and die this way." And then he felt bad that he was thinking about himself and Betty would come awake and tell him that she loved him and everything would be fine for a while. Until it started all over again.

When his shift was over Herman oftentimes went to the barn, away from everyone, and he shouted at God, "Why don't you show mercy? Don't make her suffer anymore. Please God, take her."

He slammed his fists into the hay bales until his knuckles bled. He cried. He pleaded with God to take his life and spare Betty. But always he returned for his next four-hour shift and sometimes he was surprised because Lee had worked a miracle. His wife's gaunt, haggard face would be drawn into a smile. Her hair would be combed. Her eyes would sparkle.

"Herman, I'm so glad to see you," she would gush.

"You look beautiful," he lied, as he bent to kiss her on the forehead. Her skin was cool and clammy.

Christmas came and went without celebration. Herman thought it was time for Susie to leave. He took her to a neighbor, Bill Steppe, who had a daughter Susie's age. On the way over Susie asked, "If Jubilee died where would she go?"

Herman's mind was elsewhere. Susie tried again, "Daddy, where would Jubilee go?"

"What?" said Herman. "What are you talking about? Jubilee

isn't going anywhere."

Susie had his attention. It seemed as if this were the first time she had had his undivided attention in a very long time. "If Jubilee died where would she go?"

"Nowhere."

"What do you mean, nowhere?"

"Outer space, I guess," said Herman. He was on his four hours off and did not want to think about dying. He did not want to be having this discussion.

"Where will Mommy go when she dies?"

"She will go to heaven. Straight to heaven." He thought he was going to break down and cry. He did not want to cry in front of Susie.

"Why can't Jubilee go to heaven?"

"Jubilee doesn't have a soul."

They had arrived at Steppes. Susie picked up her suitcase and got out of the car. The last words she spoke to her father were, "I don't believe you, Daddy. When you die you will find Jubilee in heaven and Mommy will be riding her." She slammed the door and stomped away.

The last day of the year was cold but the sun was shining. Betty was sitting up in bed and she looked more alert than she had in several weeks. Herman said, "It's a beautiful day. Would you like to go for a drive, Sweetie?"

Betty said, "Drive around and take a look at the country? That would be fun."

Lee questioned Herman, "Do you really think you should?"

"Yes, I do," he responded. He turned down the covers. Betty looked so small in bed. He slipped his arms under her and lifted. She seemed as light as a feather duster. He packed her to the car. Lee was already there with the door open and a blanket draped over one arm. After Herman propped Betty in the seat Lee tucked the blanket securely around her.

Herman drove into the valley. Betty was looking at things, turning her head this way and that as if she were having a difficult time focusing on any one thing. Suddenly it hit Herman. All this pain and suffering. For what? Betty was going to die anyway. A man would kill a sick animal rather than watch it suffer. Allowing a human to suffer was so unnatural. So inhumane. So cruel.

Something snapped in Herman. His rational thought processes swirled and plummeted into a black void. His hands began to shake on the wheel. He felt singularly alone in his misery, and though he wanted to chase these personal demons away, he became acutely conscious of the increasing pressure on the bottom of his right foot as he pressed down on the accelerator. The Pontiac responded. When he glanced at the speedometer it indicated they were traveling at 80 miles an hour. Ahead a juniper tree loomed like an inviting solution that would bring an abrupt end to all the problems, and pain, and suffering. He was willing to die for Betty. To die with Betty. And he might very well have carried through with his misdeed and veered into the thick trunk and the gnarled branches except at that precise instant, Betty spoke.

"Herman, don't you think you're driving a little fast?" She was looking at him, through him it seemed.

His demons flew away like so many birds after a gunshot. He lifted his foot off the gas but his hands continued to grip the steering wheel, as if that act somehow kept him anchored to this world. The Pontiac coasted harmlessly past the juniper and continued on. Herman was embarrassed and ashamed but Betty reached over and placed one of her hands, mostly skin and bone and blue veins, on his leg. She patted the leg.

"It's all right, darling," she said. "We better get back. We don't want Lee and Ray to worry."

At ten minutes to ten, on the morning of January 1, 1966, Herman sat on the edge of the bed. Betty reached out and her hand tenderly brushed against the stubble on Herman's face. She breathed, "You need a shave, Buster."

Herman smiled. He looked at her and saw the girl who had captured his heart, the woman he had shared life with, the woman he would love forever. Betty's eyelids fluttered and slowly closed. The muscles in her face relaxed. A calm, peaceful look came over her. The last words she spoke were, "Oh Herman, it's so beautiful." Herman felt the blood rush to his face. He knew she was seeing the hereafter, and that it looked an awful lot like Steele Swamp and the Devil's Garden.

THE END

EPILOGUE

We buried Betty on January 4, 1966. It was a cold, miserable day with snow on the ground and a storm blowing out of the west. A lot of folks braved the weather. They wanted to pay their last respects to a wonderful lady, a special friend.

I knew that without Betty my life was never going to be the same. But I had Susie. I had to be strong for her. She kept me going. She helped with the chores, the housework, the cooking. Every Saturday evening we treated ourselves to a restaurant meal, driving 20 miles to Ester's Cafe in Bonanza. Ester Brown put on a smorgasbord that was out of this world. It was there I became reacquainted with Jean McFall. She had lost her husband about the same time I lost Betty. We had a lot in common and before long she was joining us for dinner.

I never expected to get remarried but being with Jean seemed real natural-like. She had a background in ranching, liked the same things I did and we enjoyed each other's company. Eventually we tied the knot. Having already raised two daughters, and done a fine job with them, Jean was the perfect mother for Susie. She was kind and generous but she knew when and where to draw the line. Susie graduated from high school and went out to forge a life on her own. Jean died in July 1995.

Through the good times and the bad, Ray was always a part of the family. We lived together and worked together. We built a roping arena on our ranch in Malin and held jackpot ropings and roping schools. They became popular affairs and ropers thought nothing of driving a thousand miles to attend a weekend event. We hosted professional clinics put on by Mike Beers, where PRCA members could fine tune their skills. And we had schools for the young up-and-comers as well as those who had never picked up a rope but had a hankering to rope a steer.

Ray and I always did love kids. I couldn't begin to count how many we encouraged and schooled in the sport of roping but it must have been hundreds. Every year we brought in a group of handicapped kids from Klamath Falls. Ray and I would buy them all hats and, with a lot of volunteer help, we had every last one of them ride a horse before the day was out. You never saw kids so tickled.

Most of the time a regular buckaroo is a little tight with his emotions but kids wear their emotions on their sleeves. That's what Ray and I liked about working with kids, being a part of their joy and enthusiasm. Some have come back years later just to thank us.

I lost Ray in February 1999. Bad heart. It just gave out on him. To be perfectly honest, it has been mighty difficult on me with Ray gone. Buckarooing ain't the same any more. When I'm out in the open moving cattle I think about him. I miss his companionship something terrible. We used to get up before daylight. Ray would fix sourdough pancakes and we'd have breakfast and talk about what horses we were fixin' to ride and what we were going to do that day. Now I've got no one to talk with and it gets mighty lonesome of the mornings.

My time is coming. I know that. Nobody lives forever. When I'm gone I just hope people remember a story or two I might have told, the way I laugh — some say I cackle — and the fact I enjoyed every single day I had coming. Enjoyed it to the fullest. God gave me this life and allowed me to live it as a buckaroo. He gave me people to love and people who loved me. Can't ask for any more than that now, can you?

Herman Vowell

RICK STEBER

Rick Steber is best known for writing honest stories about the strong people and untamed landscapes of the West. His words bring readers the fragrance of sage, the views of distant plateaus and the feel of gritty desert sand between their teeth.

Rick has won numerous awards and honors for his books and his writing. He is a member of the Western Writers of America as well as the Outdoor Writers of America and has worked with the U.S. Department of Education to set national educational standards and achievement levels for U.S. history curriculum.

In addition to his writing, Rick is an engaging Western personality and is in great demand as a featured speaker at national and international conferences and banquets. He donates many hours visiting schools; talking to students about the importance of education, helping them develop reading and writing skills, and impressing upon them the value of saving our history for future generations.